ASIAN ARGUMENTS

Asian Arguments is a series of short books about Asia today. Aimed
at the growing number of students and general readers who want to
know more about the region, these books will highlight community
involvement from the ground up in issues of the day usually discussed by authors in terms of top-down government policy. The aim
is to better understand how ordinary Asian citizens are confronting
problems such as the environment, democracy and their societies'
development, either with or without government support. The books
are scholarly but engaged, substantive as well as topical, and written
by authors with direct experience of their subject matter.

ABOUT THE AUTHOR

KERRY BROWN is Senior Fellow on the Asia Programme at Chatham House, London, and Research Associate at the Centre for International Studies and Diplomacy, the School of Oriental and African Studies, London. He is author of *The Purge of the Inner Mongolian People's Party* (2006), *Struggling Giant: China in the 21st Century* (2007), *The Rise of the Dragon* (2008) and *Friends and Enemies: The Past, Present and Future of the Communist Party of China* (2009). His book *China 2020* is forthcoming. He is currently working on a political biography of Hu Jintao.

BALLOT BOX CHINA

Grassroots democracy in the final major one-party state

KERRY BROWN

Zed Books

LONDON & NEW YORK

To Claude Zanardi

Ballot Box China: Grassroots Democracy in the Final Major One Party State
was first published in 2011 by Zed Books Ltd, 7 Cynthia Street, London
N1 9JF, UK and Room 400, 175 Fifth Avenue, New York, NY 10010, USA

www.zedbooks.co.uk

Copyright © Kerry Brown 2011

FSC
www.fsc.org
MIX
Paper from
responsible sources
FSC® C013604

Typeset in Monotype Bulmer by illuminati, Grosmont
Index by John Barker
Cover designed by www.alice-marwick.co.uk
Printed and bound in Great Britain by
CPI Antony Rowe, Chippenham and Eastbourne

Distributed in the USA exclusively by Palgrave Macmillan, a division of
St Martin's Press, LLC, 175 Fifth Avenue, New York, NY 10010, USA

A catalogue record for this book is available from the British Library
Library of Congress Cataloging in Publication Data available

ISBN 978 1 84813 819 3 hb
ISBN 978 1 84813 820 9 pb
ISBN 978 1 84813 821 6 eb

Contents

Acknowledgements

I am grateful to the many people I spoke to in China while undertaking the research for this book. For reasons which will become apparent, I have kept their identities confidential. I would also like to thank Richard Youngs at the Fride Institute in Barcelona for funding much of the research on which this work is based. Paul French has been immensely supportive, in both coming up with the original idea and then guiding it through.

Abbreviations

CASS	Chinese Academy of Social Sciences
CCP	Chinese Communist Party
CCPPC	Chinese Consultative People's Political Congress
CDP	China Democracy Party
CMC	Central Military Commission
CPCC	Communist Party Central Committee
DPRK	Democratic People's Republic of Korea (North Korea)
EU	European Union
GONGO	government-organised non-governmental organisation
IP	intellectual property
KMT	Kuomintang
NDRC	National Development and Reform Council
NGO	non-governmental organisation
NPC	National People's Congress
PLA	People's Liberation Army
PRC	People's Republic of China
PSB	Public Security Bureau
RMB	renminbi (yuan)
SOE	state-owned enterprise
TVE	town and village enterprise
UNDP	United Nations Development Programme
USSR	Union of Soviet Socialist Republics
WTO	World Trade Organization

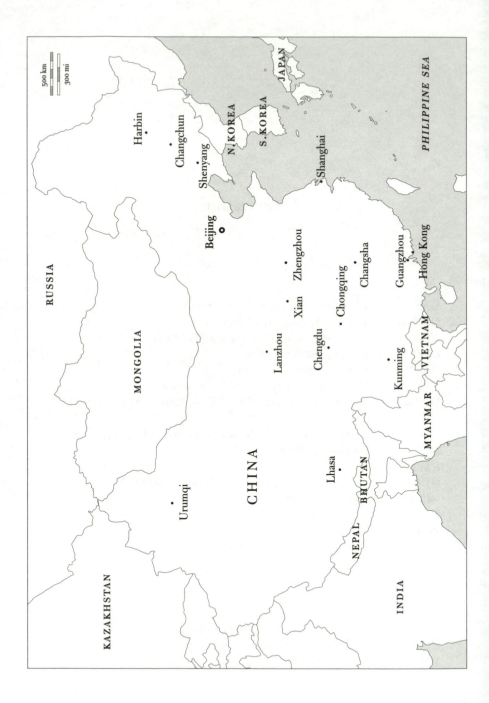

Introduction

According to its own constitution, passed in 1982 and based largely on that of the Soviet Union in the 1930s during the dark years of the Stalinist purges, the People's Republic of China (PRC) is a 'socialist state under the people's democratic dictatorship led by the working class and based on the alliance of workers and peasants'. Article 2 states that 'all power in the PRC belongs to the people'.[1] Yet in the US Department of State *2008 Human Rights Report* on China, the government structure is described as 'an authoritarian state in which the Chinese Communist Party (CCP) constitutionally is the paramount source of power'. These two perspectives show the clash between how China describes itself and how it is seen from outside.

This book looks at the issue of how democracy is being introduced and promoted in the world's last major state in which a Communist Party holds a monopoly of power. According to Oxford professor Archie Brown, in his *The Rise and Fall of Communism*, there are now only five countries left with such a system. The others are Cuba, Laos, Vietnam and North Korea. The PRC is in a different league to these in terms of size and influence. I will argue that village democracy offers a key way in which to see this great attempted transformation. Village democracy raises many issues intimately related to sustainable governance and stability in China and reflects on a micro-level the kinds of challenges and changes that the country will have to go through in order to have a chance of surviving as a centralised, stable and economically successful modern state. In that sense what is happening in the countryside is not only interesting but highly meaningful.

For China can claim that it is in fact already a democracy, at least at the village level. Since the 1980s, it has held elections that have many of the characteristics of those in democracies in the West. There have been more candidates than positions to be filled. The ballots have been one person, one vote, and they have been secret. There have been campaigns with public announcements of the victors. And, perhaps most crucial of all, some of those who have stood and won in these elections have not needed to be Communist Party members.

Since the first formal national law allowing these elections in 1988 China has held almost a million of them in 600,000 villages. It has done this in order to give some accountability and stability to governance in over 800,000 villages in the country. But, as this book will show, the results have been mixed. And the impact is still hard to judge. Some have seen this as a massive educational process, getting many millions of Chinese used to the ideas of democratic process. But others have seen it as a cynical manoeuvre to allow the upper levels of the Communist Party to achieve at least some legitimacy through Village Party committees, which until quite recently were largely there to implement the state's dirty work – enforcing the one-child policy and collecting taxes. As this book aims to show, in this vast exercise in introducing notions of accountability and competition into public governance, some areas have succeeded and others have spectacularly failed. Academics and officials in China have been divided between those who see this as a major step forward in the way the PRC is governed and those who look upon it as an unnecessary and destabilising viral infection introduced from the West, creating more problems than it solves.

As of the time of writing this book, the original speculation over a decade ago that the central government in Beijing was about to launch a huge new series of elections on the village model to higher levels of government, such as townships and above, has been disproved. Village elections are stuck firmly where they have been for some years, with no sign at all that the Beijing leaders are going to roll them out to more ambitious areas any time soon. As of 2010 no official in China with significant powers of decision-making over the deployment of resources is publicly elected. Many commentators and supporters of liberal democracy continue to wait for the day when that happens, and when therefore China can be said to have moved much more dramatically towards a form of democracy that is similar to that which exists in most of the developed world, and in much of the developing world, if indeed that ever happens. Current elite leaders of the CCP have consistently stated that they are not interested in Western models of democracy. This will be discussed in the chapters that follow.

This book looks at the issue of elections in China in a very practical way. There has been much good technical work on elections in terms of analysis and description. But here I have tried to tell as accessibly as I can the story of elections and reactions to them through individuals and commentators. For those seeking more detailed treatment of the various aspects of rural democracy I have added a bibliography with some suggestions for further reading. Chapter 1 supplies context, looking at the ways in which historically China has had elections and what the roots of a kind of democratic system in the country are. Some of this material pre-dates the foundation of the PRC in 1949. Chapter 2 looks at the understanding of democracy that exists now. As a word, 'democracy' is increasingly popular even among the political elite in the PRC, along with this puzzling concept of 'democracy with Chinese characteristics'. This chapter attempts to explain a little of what might be behind this language, and why the concept is framed in the way it is.

Chapter 3 looks at the village election process, how elections are held in villages, who can stand in them, how they are conducted, and what their outcomes are. This provides an overview of the rich experience of holding elections over the last two decades, with some data on how many have been held, where, how many candidates, and who has won. Chapter 4 assesses the problems and challenges this enormous exercise has thrown up, specifically through the separate voices of those directly related to the whole process, from officials to academics, to policy advisers. Chapter 5 sets the process in its larger context, discussing how it forms part of a constellation of issues, from legal reform to the creation of non-governmental organisations, and civil society, to strategies to deal with political opposition. I then finally look to the future, setting out where this process stands today, what plans there are, and, most crucially, how they will impact on the far larger issue of China's overall political and administrative reform in the coming two decades. My conclusion is that China faces immense challenges in the way in which it governs itself in the short- to medium-term future, and has to make some enormous and bold decisions about how to transform its system to something more representative, less centralised and more participatory. While Western liberal democratic models may not be wholly appropriate, it is clear that somehow China will need to move from the model of governance it has now to something that is more fit for purpose for the highly modernised, complex economy and society that it has. Successfully undergoing this transition will be a massive challenge, fraught with risks. On its success or failure depends much of the world's economic and political security in the decades ahead.

1

A brief history of elections, democracy and civil society in modern China

We have been told on innumerable occasions and in innumerable sources in English, Chinese and other languages that China has no history of democracy. One of the most forceful proponents of this view is the current leadership elite in Beijing. To the Communists democracy is a promise, which stands many decades down the line, after China has become a strong, wealthy country, and 'improved the quality' of its people.

The Communists have aggressively promoted a narrative supporting this in which the long sweep of Chinese history has been characterised as 'feudalistic' from the earliest dynasties, over four millennia ago, down to the fall of the Qing Dynasty in 1911–12. Using templates largely borrowed from Marx, the class struggle has continued throughout the centuries between an imperial court elite based in the various shifting capitals of multiple predecessor countries and states that existed before the creation of the People's Republic of China (PRC) and the vast majority of the population, divided between landowners, usually small ones, farmers and peasants. Lacking any meaningful industrialisation while Europe and North America were undergoing the first Industrial Revolution, China remained a country based on an agrarian economy deep into the twentieth century. Social relations were seen as being overwhelmingly exploitative, with the Communists talking in the early years of their revolution of 'a dog eat dog society' where the peasant and working class fed the elite with their sweat and blood.

After the fall of the Qing in 1911, Republican China undertook a series of political and economic reforms which were meant to drag the country into the twentieth century, establishing at least some industrial capacity in urban centres like Shanghai. By 1920, however, of a population of over 400 million, only 2 million were categorised as proletarian. While Qing-era economic activity had involved surprising levels of sophisticated artisanship,[1] by 1930 there was little proper infrastructure, and a largely stagnant industrial base. Severe political instability and disunity did not help things. Tragically, what had been built in the first quarter of a century of Republican rule was blown away by the devastating Sino–Japanese war from 1937 onwards. Tellingly, China's victimisation was at the hands of the one Asian power that had managed so far to adopt a Western industrial model and gain from it. This was not lost on China's intellectual elite.

The May 4th Movement of 1919 (see below) celebrated the twin hopes of 'Mr Science' and 'Mr Democracy'. This slogan was to echo hauntingly across the ensuing decades. A student uprising, mostly taking place in Beijing, it had been caused initially by the ceding of German's concessions in North East China to Japan as a result of the Versailles Treaty at the end of the First World War. In July 1921, largely as an offshoot of the intellectual ferment which had produced the 4 May events, the Communist Party under the tutelage of the International Comintern of the Soviet Union held its First Congress in Shanghai. But with only a few dozen members the Chinese Communists were doomed to an early history scarred by struggle, setbacks and tragedy, not the least of which was their near annihilation in the main urban base for their activity, Shanghai, in April 1927, when General Chiang Kai-shek, the de facto leader of China at the time, ordered a murderous purge. Over 5,000 were to die. The Communists disappeared into the countryside from this point, radically changing their strategy, recruiting among the peasantry rather than the cities, and articulating a new form of communism under the increasingly charismatic leadership of Mao Zedong.

Early elections

Whatever forms of government existed in China prior to 1911, and however they represented the various views of key segments of society before then, elections did not play a part. In that sense, there was no history, as in England for instance, of elites and sub-elites asserting their rights against kings and emperors and creating chambers for decision-making and a legal framework to support these rights. Even when the first hint of modernisation appeared in the middle of the nineteenth century when the Qing court had its first uncomfortable and unsuccessful encounter with Western imperialists like Great Britain, the USA and Germany, there was no thought of creating upper and lower chambers, and having representatives for regions elected by populations. At most an ancient system existed in which petitions were submitted from subjects to the imperial centre, a system that still exists in the twenty-first century under the new political order. The country was in effect run by a system of provincial and central bureaucracy, with an elite of mandarins who were in charge of everything from collection of taxes to the titles of land. The power system was utterly vertical, with an almost infinite distance between the emperor and his subjects. Some would argue that this too has remained a feature of the post-revolutionary order.

In the late Qing, reformists influenced by exposure to foreign ideas, like Kang Youwei and Liang Qichao,[2] in a late burst of activity urged radical change on the imperial system, bringing in modernisation and reform. But, as the title of their movement suggests, the '100 days reforms' were short-lived. Only violent upheaval and revolution would finally remove the old elite and bring in new rulers. In 1912,

China had its first and so far only national election (see 'China's first election' below). But it was to end quickly. By the end of the decade China had split into a number of competing territories where all-powerful warlords competed against each other and the central government exercised hardly any control.

China's first election

In the chaotic aftermath of the military uprising that created the Republic of China in 1911–12 and felled the Qing Dynasty after more than 260 years in power, China did something it had never done before, and has not (so far) since – held a national election. The main party contending this was the Nationalists (KMT), founded only a few months before from what was originally the Tongmenghui, a group agitating for the overthrow of the Qing, and a coalition of smaller parties. According to the constitution of the provisional national government, elections were to be held to decide on a bicameral national assembly. This existed in parallel to the office of a country president, who at that time was one of the main military leaders, Yuan Shi-kai.

Song Jiaoren, a returnee from Japan, and widely recognised as the founder of the KMT alongside Dr Sun Yat-sen, led the party in these elections against a number of other parties, including the Unification Party, the Republican Party and the Democratic Party. The elections were held in February 1913, and led to a clear victory for the KMT, which took 269 seats out of 596 in the upper house, and 123 out of 274 in the lower. Song campaigned largely on the back of criticism of the increasingly autocratic leadership style of Yuan, and the suggestion that China was rapidly sliding back to the same kind of monarchical system it had just managed to liberate itself from. But Song's political ambitions were cut brutally short. As he was preparing to become the new premier of China, on his way from Shanghai to Beijing in March 1913 he was assassinated. He was only 31. While never conclusively confirmed, the main suspicion falls on Yuan, who had dealt with other opponents in a similar fashion. The assassin died in prison before coming to trial. Yuan himself was to survive until 1916. He died only a few months after declaring himself emperor.[3]

One of the largely forgotten democratic legacies was provincial elections held in the 1930s. Frank Dikötter has uncovered these in his study of the period before Mao. The Republican period, he states, was 'politically more democratic than many comparable regimes in Europe at the time or than the People's Republic has been'.[4] The City Council in foreign-controlled Shanghai in the first decades of the twentieth century was democratic, with a division between executive and legislative branches. By as early as 1907, anyone resident in the city for over five years was entitled to vote. By 1912, 40 million people were able to select members of the National Assembly and the House of Representatives (see box). Provincial elections in 1918 involved over 36 million people.[5] Provinces like Hunan and Zhejiang in the 1910s and 1920s introduced voting rights across society, with the establishment of the Democratic League in 1941, and organisations to protect civil and legal rights. From 1929 onwards the Nationalist government also introduced village elections, something the Communists would wait for three decades to do after 1949.

In other parts of the country, from Manchuria to Nanjing, varied forms of universal-suffrage elections were held for local assemblies. Further elections were held for the National Assembly in May 1936. Carl Crow, the US businessman based long-term in Shanghai, stated that by 1944 China had become 'a nation which will carry the light of democracy to the millions of East Asia'.[6] This was connected to the rich, complex movements of a free press, and to civil society groups in Nationalist China. Civil society groups in particular had a vigorous life, especially those connected with trade, religion and social movements. 'Associations and institutions that engaged in political, social or cultural activities outside of state control had deep roots prior to the establishment of the PRC in 1949', writes Qiusha Ma in a study of non-governmental organisations (NGOs) in China.[7] She looks in particular at Chambers of Commerce and intellectual associations which started to exist in the final period of the Qing era but then came into their own from the May 4th Movement in 1919 onwards (see box below). The statistics she provides are impressive. By 1915 there were 1,242 Chambers of Commerce.[8] In 1911 there were 500 newspapers nationwide, with a readership of 42 million, approximately 10 per cent of China's population at this time.[9] 'The new institutions demonstrated a certain degree of democratic and voluntary nature'[10] with leaders of Chambers of Commerce elected. The Red Cross and other international civil society groups were all eventually represented in Republican China.

The May 4th Movement, 1919

Despite marking both the sixtieth anniversary of the founding of the PRC and the twentieth anniversary of the Tiananmen Square uprising in 1989, 2009 was also significant for being the ninetieth anniversary of one of the seminal protests of the twentieth century – the May 4th Movement, which occurred largely in Beijing and Shanghai in 1919. It was provoked by protests at the 'shameful settlement that China had been forced to accept at the Paris Peace Conference which had ended World War 1'.[11] Under the terms of the Treaty of Versailles, those territories that had been under German sovereignty were given to Japan, and not handed back to China. Thousands demonstrated in anger at this continuation of their humiliation at the hands of foreigners. From 1919 onwards social movements in China became much more energised by the desire to assert China's self-interest, to strengthen it, and to deal with some of the historic roots of its problems – in particular the highly hierarchical, conservative tradition of Confucianism. Rana Mitter, Professor of the History and Politics of Modern China at Oxford University, has described the movement which spread from the events of May 1919 as being derived from 'a group of Chinese thinkers [feeling] that something was holding their country back from combating evils such as imperialism and warlordism'. Their answer was to blame 'traditional Chinese culture, based on the philosophy of Confucius'.[12] Two of the slogans that were used after the May 4th Movement were 'Mr Science' and 'Mr Democracy'. These were to be repeated as Chinese, especially young Chinese intellectuals, wrestled with the modernisation of their country, and its best future political form, in the ensuing decades. But from 1949, they also became something of an accusation, showing that China had failed to live up to the high expectations of change and reform in the early decades of the twentieth century. China continues to wrestle with some of the legacy of the 4 May incident to this day, and the event occupies a hallowed place in the universe of anniversaries faithfully kept in the PRC. If there is such a thing as a Chinese democratic tradition, then its roots reach back to 4 May 1919, and it has been an event which has inspired activists as disparate as Wei Jingsheng in his 'Fifth Modernisation' demand after the Democracy Wall Movement in 1979 and the Tiananmen Square protesters in 1989.

Meltdown

As Marx famously commented, history is written by the victors. This is part of the reason why the Chinese Republican era gets a very bad press. Blamed for venality, corruption and the final implosion of China, Chiang Kai-shek and his army fled to the island of Taiwan, where in 1949 they established the Republic of China on Taiwan, which exists to this day. The victorious Communists were able to set about rubbishing their almost fifty-year-long record of rule on the mainland, producing strong denunciations and dismissals of all that they had done. Only in the last two decades has there been a more measured attempt among PRC scholars to judge the Republican period. Biographies in particular of Chiang Kai-shek have appeared in mainland bookshops, and he has been represented as a leader who, at least in his early period, stood up for the Chinese national interest.

Whatever the nascent infrastructure of democratic institutions and processes, at national and local level, along with civil society and media, these were to be brutally swept away as a result of the Sino–Japanese war. From 1931 China was to be the object of increasingly aggressive behaviour by the Japanese. By 1937 this had become all-out conflict. The poets W.H. Auden and Christopher Isherwood recorded their journey into China at about this time. Preoccupied with their first encounter with a strange and different culture, much of their account, published afterwards, is about their meetings with exotic, interesting people, and their frustrations in travelling into a country with which they were unfamiliar, and the language and customs of which they did not know. But the escalating war encroaches into their good-humoured account, so that they can record at the end that 'In this city [Hong Kong], conquered, yet unoccupied by its conquerors, the mechanism of the old life is still ticking, but seems doomed to stop, like a watch dropped in the desert.'[13] The same year of their visit, Nanjing was attacked, and many thousands murdered and raped by Japanese troops. While Western journalists present in the city recorded the devastation (one, Till Durdin, wrote in the *New York Times* that 'wholesale looting, the violation of women, the murder of civilians, the eviction of Chinese from their homes, mass execution of war prisoners' were some of the evils perpetuated over the weeks of the carnage[14]), Japanese journalists present began a long history of denying that anything had happened at all.[15] To this day, a strong constituency in Japan continues to dispute the Nanjing massacre, causing much bad feeling between Japan and China. The rest of the war was to have an indisputable impact, leading to 20 million Chinese dead and over 70 million displaced. In order to counter the invasion and occupation, the Nationalists under Chiang Kai-shek and the Communist Party, founded in 1921 and slowly emerging as one of the key political forces of rural China (somewhat ironic, in view of orthodox Marxism's insistence that revolution needed to be first waged in the cities), formed a United Front, pooling their military capacity and fighting the Japanese across the war front running approximately straight down the middle of the country.

The Japanese were defeated but at fearsome cost. And the China that emerged had most of its industrial infrastructure blown away, with its cities and economy left in a ruinous state. A further three years of civil war between the KMT and the Communists, as a result of their failure to reach a political settlement at the end of the 1945 ceasefire, only left things more ruinous. In 1949, the KMT, whose armies after all had done most to win the battles against the Japanese (the CCP contribution was crucial in certain sectors, but still less than that of the KMT), were facing raging inflation, powerful public anger at corruption, and failure in military encounters with the Communists. The PRC was founded on 1 October 1949.

It is one of history's great 'what ifs' to speculate what might have happened to the governance of China had the Japanese not invaded, and the country been left to travel a more peaceful path. Would the signs of more democratic governance have been allowed to flourish, and to create the sort of institutions and systems that came to exist eventually in other developing countries in the region, like South Korea, India and Japan? So profound was the influence of the war on destroying the old world, and creating a new, more polarised one, that it is hard to imagine how things would have developed without it. But the economic record of the Nationalists at least up to 1937 was improving, and there were signs that reforms would have happened both in the area of governance and in society. Even the dominant leader of the Communists from 1938 onwards, Mao Zedong, had low expectations of them ever being anything more than a minority political force in society, right up to the eve of eventual victory over the Nationalists in 1949. In 1972, he was to thank the first visiting prime minister of Japan to Beijing since 1949 for helping to radicalise the Chinese people and push more of them to supporting the CCP's cause.

Mao, the Communists and democracy

With the ascendancy of the Communists within China, a whole new understanding of political processes and of democracy was introduced into the country. Inevitably this became dominant after

1949. There were many areas in which the Communists did not introduce widespread changes as had been expected. Their policy, for instance, on national minority issues, on Tibet, Xinjiang and other border areas, was, despite earlier promises, almost exactly the same as that of the Nationalists. Plans to create a 'federated China' in the 1940s were replaced by the more loaded notion of 'liberating' areas like Tibet once the CCP had come to power. In this area,

> despite the party's persistent claim that its revolution would destroy the 'old China' and create a 'new' one, in terms of how to define China, its leadership's way of thinking demonstrated a remarkable continuity with that of the Nationalists, the political reigning force of the 'old China' that the Party had strived to overthrow.[16]

In social policy, they did clear up some of the 'bad forces' that had existed under the Nationalists, with huge campaigns against landowners, mafia groups and pimps. Their main target was capitalist forces, who were blamed for the profound inequalities that had developed in China in the last century, with responsibility being pinned on foreign exploitation and internal corruption.

In addition to creating a form of Marxism–Leninism that was suitable for China's largely agricultural economy, Mao had been working since the early 1930s on the correct labelling of class forces in society and on the sort of political structures that would strengthen and liberate China. 'A lively atmosphere has prevailed throughout the country ever since the War of Resistance began', Mao wrote in 1940 from his isolated base in North China, in an essay entitled 'On New Democracy': 'There is a general feeling that a way out of the impasse has been found, and people no longer knit their brows in despair.'[17] Referring to the need to 'seek truth from facts', Mao then sketched out what the new democracy in China would look like.

Mao's great genius was to relate generic communist ideology to the specific conditions prevailing in rural China, where almost 90 per cent of Chinese still lived. To these people talk of constructing an industrial-based proletariat made no sense. If this were ever to happen it would be decades in the future (only in 2010 did Chinese rural and urban populations finally equal out). Revolutionary change was needed now. The question was how:

> For many years we Communists have struggled for a cultural revolution as well as for a political and economic revolution, and our aim is to build a new society and a new state for the Chinese nation. That new society and new state will have not only a new politics and a new economy but a new culture. In other words, not only do we want to change a China that is politically oppressed and economically exploited into a China that is politically free and economically prosperous, we also want to change the China which is being kept ignorant and backward under the sway of the old culture into an enlightened and progressive China under the sway of a new culture. In short, we want to build a new China. Our aim in the cultural sphere is to build a new Chinese national culture.[18]

New democracy in Mao's vision was linked to China's historic circumstances of feudalism and deep inequality, the global revolution which was being waged via the Communist Party and the International Comintern of the Soviet Union, and the unity between newly emerging social forces in China – the proletariat, the peasantry, the intelligentsia and other sections of the petty bourgeoisie:

> The Chinese democratic republic which we desire to establish now must be a democratic republic under the joint dictatorship of all anti-imperialist and anti-feudal people led by the proletariat, that is, a new-democratic republic, a republic of the genuinely revolutionary new Three People's Principles with their Three Great Policies.

This would look 'different to the European American form of capitalist republic under a bourgeois dictatorship'. Such a democracy would, as had been promised in the USSR, deliver power to the people, and make them masters of their own affairs.

This in essence was the political programme that Mao and his fellow leaders introduced in the PRC after 1949. The CCP and the National People's Congress (NPC) were seen as the fundamental expressions of the people's power. An ideology was built up around this. The infrastructure of elections, different political parties, and potential sources of power that lay beyond the control of the CCP such as they existed in Republican China were removed. The CCP came to dominate the key areas of people's political, legal and, increasingly, intellectual and social life.

Democracy under Mao appears to have been, and was, a paradox. As his period in power continued, it was centralised, concentrated increasingly in the hands of a few people, and finally existed almost solely under his control. This clearly was not the intention in the early years of the PRC when the CCP went out of its way to recruit representatives across society, creating various consultative groups and attempting to engage people at all levels of society in the project to modernise and industrialise China. But by the Cultural Revolution from 1967 onwards, dictatorship became the more common expression, and what little signs of democracy there had been were submerged. The eight patriotic parties, all of them founded before 1949, were allowed to exist but within a space carefully delineated by the CCP. The NPC and Chinese Consultative People's Political Congress (CCPPC) became servants of the CCP's whims (see Chapter 2). The trade unions and civil society groups were purged of their independence and largely infiltrated with Party representatives to lead them, having only a shadow existence as time went on. The CCP subscribed to the orthodox Marxist belief that religion was no more than a form of ideological control by oppressive ruling elites before liberation and therefore needed to be expunged. Non-state economic activity was almost wholly eliminated by 1956. The CCP set up in the space of only a decade an astonishing infrastructure of control – social, educational and institutional. Legal processes, whatever had started to exist in the Republican period, were stifled so that by the death of Mao in 1976 there existed no meaningful law courts or process of law to speak of. All this had to be rebuilt from 1978, and is continuing to this day. As the culmination of this centralisation of power and concentration in the hands of one despotic individual, by the end of the 1960s even the CCP itself became the victim of Mao's own megalomania, with him sponsoring wholesale purges of the Party at national and provincial levels, felling swathes of his former comrades, and supporting Red Guards and rebellious groups as they unleashed terror on those who had formerly been leaders.[19]

The Cultural Revolution remains one of the most perplexing events in modern Chinese history, despite a voluminous literature trying to explain and document it in Chinese and other languages. The CCP's own formal judgement on the causes of the Cultural Revolution, issued in 1981, states that the event was 'initiated and led by Comrade Mao Zedong'. During the Cultural Revolution, 'we [CCP leaders] substantially broadened the scope of class struggle'. This was adjudged an error, leading to social chaos and instability. But, as Roderick Macfarquhar and Michael Schoenhals have written in their history of this period, the more salient explanation was the concentration of frightening amounts of power in the hands of one man. During the period of the Cultural Revolution 'The Chairman [Mao]'s prestige grew, and his arrogance alongside it. He gradually acted more and more arbitrarily, increasingly putting himself above the Party's central committee [its formal leadership body] … The fact remains', they ruefully conclude, 'that Party leaders of considerable ability, experience, toughness and prestige failed – all of them – to struggle against an 'emperor' when he ran amok'.[20]

The 'decade of chaos', as it was subsequently called, did have two highly paradoxical outcomes, however, that are pertinent to the wider issue of the democratisation of China and the appearance of village elections a decade later. The first was that this era, with its chaos, saw the appearance of a whole range of semi-democratic groups and publications, which, while they were unified in their agreement on the centrality of Mao Zedong and his greatness, often agreed about precious little else. There were battles between those who believed in a hereditary view of class and those who believed in more mobility; between those who believed in a stronger role for the military and those who opposed this; and between those who believed in fiercer attacks on the Soviet Union and other neighbours and those who resisted this. Over the period of the Cultural Revolution some tough questions were asked of Chinese society, and many of its less pleasant divisions and fractures were revealed. In particular, virulent campaigns were waged against ethnic minorities and other socially excluded groups. It is possible, therefore, because of this contention and competition between different rebellious groups, to talk of a perverse kind of Cultural Revolution democracy.

More concretely, the Cultural Revolution took a terrible toll on social stability in China, leading to 'chaos, killing, and, at the end ... stagnation' and costing China 'well over a year's worth of national income'.[21] Many parts of the country descended into lawlessness, with barely any institutions functioning. This reached such a parlous state that, by 1969, only the military were able to restore order. Schools and universities closed down. Students were allowed to roam about the country free, agitating for revolution. Even central government ministries were unable to function. At the basic countryside level, some village areas descended into squalid barbarity. Historian and author Zheng Yi records only the most horrific of these, the incidence of cannibalism in the south-west province of Guangxi.[22] The great modernist writer Lu Xun had written about a society where men would eat men; in the Maoist period, villagers were reduced to just such a state. Large parts of Inner Mongolia were so badly affected by purges of cadres of Mongolian ethnicity that there were few areas of activity, economic, political or social, that functioned in the worst years from 1967 to 1969.

The Chinese countryside: home to China's sorrow

Tragically, the rural plight during the Cultural Revolution came at the end of a period of devastation for the countryside. The combination of lawlessness and economic mismanagement from 1949 onwards in rural China were the driving factors behind the introduction of elections after 1978. This at least gave governance in villages some semblance of legitimacy and popular support.

While the Cultural Revolution had a deep impact on governance in villages, this came after the impact of the Great Leap Forward and the vast famines of the early 1960s. In some senses these had an even worse result. Historian Ralph A. Thaxton has dealt with this tragic history through the events that happened in one small village. The notion that there was a clean break and a fresh beginning for peasants and farmers after 1949 was not so straightforward: 'The pre-1949 Maoist insurgency attracted rural people from all walks of life, promising them freedom from agricultural scarcity, corrupt and violent dictatorship, and pillage, rape and murder by invading armies of various stripes. Yet the impact of state violence, famine and war led to the rise of native local Communist leaders who practiced violent politics in their home communities.'[23]

This proved incompatible with their initial promises to build democracy and good governance. This history of violence in the Chinese countryside was deep-rooted; the Communists were only continuing methods used by previous governments when they un-leashed 'unbelievable savagery in rural communities' during the early 1960s. The roots of this were the series of land ownership reorganisa-tions during the 1950s after the Communists took power, culminating in wholesale land collectivisation in 1957. People's Communes, which existed from 1958, meant that the 'party state took over all privately held farmland and draft animals'.[24] The Communes were also meant to restructure radically the balance of rural life, breaking down the traditional family framework and destroying previous power systems. The Great Leap Forward from 1959 onwards, while focused on industrial production, was also aiming to push up productivity in the agricultural sector. It was a final solution to the age-old problem of famine in Chinese society, which had left such a profound, dis-figuring scar across the centuries. But it soon became clear that the reorganisation had produced the exact opposite effect to its intention, and caused cadres, who were due to implement the new collectivist system, to come into direct conflict with farmers. By 1962 the countryside was starving in order to support the urban areas. Even more obscenely, the exporting of foodstuffs continued. 'In mid

1960, the central government launched a campaign to increase the amount of 'substitute foods' available in the countryside... For Mao, the ultimate goal ... was to make China's village people reserve as much good food grain for the state as possible so that the state could use it to provision the cities and sustain exports.'[25]

Farmers and villagers did not take this state onslaught lying down but practised a number of forms of resistance. Some subverted the collection of grain and other crops by covertly eating them early, before they were ripe for harvest. There was a booming black market, with many levels of official collusion. And a whole new area of the economy appeared, outside the reach of any formal data, where crops were grown in backyards, spare plots of land and other places in order to give at least some access to food. Before the Cultural Revolution had even started, therefore, there was a legacy of anger and bitterness in the countryside, which meant that once forces had been unleashed in 1967 officials and those seen as guilty of this earlier debacle were singled out for particularly vicious reprisals. Ironically, therefore, at the most local level the Cultural Revolution operated as an extraordinary opportunity to let off steam, and in that sense, even more paradoxically, may well have been a means of restoring at least some basic level of social stability. There were plenty of other areas, however, where disruption continued and often got worse.

The 'Great Leap disaster all but destroyed the legitimacy of the Communist Party in the countryside', which meant that 'Mao attempted to prevent any discourse about the famine'.[26] The period became a taboo subject, with the consequence that the first proper histories of what happened in the countryside then, with some estimates of the numbers of people that died, only started to appear in Chinese in the early 2000s.[27] But 'whispered' histories, those contained in oral history and in people's intimate and family memories, meant that the overwhelming tragedy of this period was never forgotten.

The memories persisted in both silent and whispered forms, keeping alive the bitter experience derived from the Great Leap engagement with Maoist state power and diluting the Party's attempt to convert the haunting dream of the famine into a non-lethal, morally ambiguous tragedy.[28]

Former Xinhua journalist and historian Yang Jisheng has only recently resurrected this true history, in his immense Chinese-language study *Tombstone* (*Mubei*), published in 2008 and then promptly banned in the mainland because of continuing sensitivities about this period of history on the part of the authorities.

Democracy Wall, the fifth modernisation and 1989

The final mystery that the Cultural Revolution throws up is the appearance in 1973, during one of the most disheartening periods of modern Chinese history, of a wall poster in Guangzhou, co-authored by three activists under the title 'On Socialist Democracy and the Chinese Legal System'. The authors chose the pen name Li Yizhe, a compound of characters from each of their names. Reacting to the recent news that Mao Zedong's chosen successor and comrade-in-arms Lin Biao was exposed as having been in fact a 'renegade and traitor', the authors 'called upon the masses to demand democracy, demand socialist legality, and revolutionary and personal rights that protect the broad masses'. Following in the footsteps of the earliest heterodox thinkers, Li Yizhe's writing also emphasised 'guaranteeing people's rights to run their own country and society, and explored ways to make government officials accountable to the people'.[29]

This belonged to a tradition of asking for more rights and countering the increasingly oppressive atmosphere of the late Maoist period. But, with decimated courts and barely functioning systems of accountability and governance, their call was a brave voice which fell on deaf ears. Highly symbolically, Zhang Zhixin, one of the martyrs of the era, was executed in 1975 for questioning Mao; her neck had been twisted so that she was unable to speak during her brief trial and her execution. Zhang Chunqiao, one of the members of the Gang of Four, was to produce the essential final statement on political structures in the dying days of the Cultural Revolution. The title of his masterpiece says it all: 'On Exercising All-Round

Dictatorship over the Bourgeoisie'.[30] Brutally silencing opposition was the method of choice until Mao's death in September 1976. Only then were the real impediments to dealing with the PRC's colossal problems of how it was ruled and how it could confront its immense challenges of stability dealt with.

The means to do this were originally through the 'Four Modernisations', articulated by Premier Zhou Enlai in 1975 while he was suffering from cancer. He was to die only a year later, but the legacy of his modernisation drive was to live on in his main political protégé, Deng Xiaoping. 'For an entire decade', Zhou's biographer Gao Wenqian records, 'a political and ideological struggle had consumed the nation. Zhou now called for China to shift its focus to the difficult but necessary tasks of modernizing its agriculture, its industry, its national defence and its fields of science and technology.'[31] These tasks at least were to provide the basis of China's new policies after 1978, opening up its economy and beginning the transformation the country has seen in the last three decades. However, even as these were being promoted and enshrined in a new raft of policies, the Democracy Wall Movement in Beijing, in the winter of 1978 and spring of 1979, was demanding that a fifth modernisation be added – democracy. The most famous exponent of this was Wei Jingsheng, who had been an electrician at Beijing Zoo. In his wall poster he stated: 'If the Chinese vote for modernization, they first must establish democracy and modernize the Chinese social system.'[32] His naming of Deng Xiaoping as a new dictator in a subsequent essay sealed his fate. The Democracy Wall Movement was shut down, and Wei imprisoned for fourteen years, a term subsequently extended for a further fourteen years before his early release and exile to the USA in 1998.

Mr Democracy's long, unfinished Chinese march

The high ambitions of those students who protested in Beijing in May 1919 calling for science and democracy were to be confronted,

over the following decades, with bloodshed, tragedy and finally
tyranny. Only in 1978 did China start to emerge from this era,
shaken and changed. But the legacy of war and Maoism needed to
be urgently addressed. Deng talked often of step-by-step reforms,
most pithily expressed in the use of the phrase, imputed to him,
to 'cross the river by feeling the stones'. Approaches to China's
condition were to be framed in two ways. The first was to deal
with the economic situation before anything else. The second was
to ensure that whatever changes were made, they would be gradual
and carefully controlled. Talk of a wholesale transformation of the
system was therefore highly premature. Bold reformers in the 1980s
were aware of the political parameters within which they needed
to work. Former Politburo Standing Committee member and vice
premier Li Langqing, in his memoirs published in English in 2009,
refers to the shift in the key focus of Chinese government policy as
a result of the 1978 Third Plenary from 'taking class struggle as the
key link' to 'developing the productive force'.[33] This meant modernising industry and introducing market reforms in China, along with
opening up to the outside world and deepening the professionalisa-
tion of Chinese human capital. Although Li does not mention him,
former CCP secretary Zhao Ziyang was to paint a similar picture of
this period, during which he played a pivotal role in the Politburo,
in his posthumous memoirs published in 2009.[34] The key issue was
to increase China's productivity and its industrial efficiency. 'The
Chinese economy was in a shambles', Li recounts,

> and people were hard up as a result of the decade-long calamity of
> the Cultural Revolution. According to the China Statistical Year
> Book statistics, China accounted for 4.7 percent of the world's
> gross domestic product (GDP) in 1955, thanks to post-Liberation
> efforts, but the figure plummeted to 1 per cent in 1978. In 1976, the
> Chinese consumed a per capita average of 190.5 kilograms of grain,
> compared with 197.5 kilograms in 1952, and workers of state-owned
> or collective firms earned an average of 575 yuan, compared with
> 583 yuan in 1966 ... 250 million rural people, for their part, were
> having trouble making ends meet.[35]

The villages were part of this. Still dominated by the vestiges of the commune system, they had become the crucible of new experiments in governance and economic productivity. Zhao Ziyang was to admit this in his own account, smuggled out of China in 2008, three years after his death. Hardly heeding central diktats, farmers grew what they wanted, and in the early 1980s started to see a market for their products. As Deng Xiaoping was to admit, 'In the rural reform our greatest success – and it is one we had by no means anticipated – has been the emergence of a large number of enterprises run by villages and townships. They were like a new force that just came into being spontaneously.'[36]

Any suggestion that what had been achieved in the economic field could be duplicated in the political field was resisted. Witness the calamity of June 1989, when students, some of whom believed that they belonged to the noble tradition of the May 4th Movement, demonstrated in central Beijing, only to be crushed by the People's Liberation Army (PLA). Demands for reform of the CCP on the same lines as had been happening in the Soviet Union and Eastern Europe were rebuffed. From the early 1990s, with the collapse of the USSR, the CCP went through a crisis, with many predicting inside and outside of China that it would follow the same course. But it maintained the strict policy of opening up the economy, while carefully restricting all moves to allow these reforms to migrate into the political control of the country. Despite its allowing private business people to join the Party from 2001 and presiding over one of the world's most vibrant and dynamic economies, as of 2011 the CCP continues to exercise as much of a monopoly on power as it did in 1949, albeit in a very different way.

How is China governed today?

To have some idea of how village elections happen, and where they fit into the system of the PRC as it stands, it is necessary to draw out the current structures of government and power. The PRC has been governed since 1949 by the CCP.

THE PARTY

The CCP remains dominant in China; although there are eight patriotic political parties, these are merely advisory and have no significant powers. The CCP and the government are, in theory, separate in China, but in fact real power remains very much in the hands of the CCP.

China is divided into thirty-one provinces, autonomous regions and city regions, directly under the central government. In each of these there are parallel structures for Party and for government. This extends right down to the lowest levels of administration in China, the villages, of which there are almost 800,000 across the country. Each of these has a Village Committee, with two or three elected members, and a Party branch with a CCP representative. At township, prefectural, provincial and national levels, the same structure pertains.

The CCP has over 76 million members. Although a large number, this accounts for only 7 per cent of China's 1.3 billion population. To join the Party, people must undertake interviews and write statements about their belief in the CCP. They are then sponsored by a couple of Party members. Party members must uphold the Party's belief system, pay a small subscription each month, and, from time to time, attend meetings about Party matters. There is also an organisation for those aged 14 to 26 called the China Youth League. This has over 84 million members.

Real power in the Party is exercised by the Central Committee. This currently has 204 full members and 164 'alternate' (or 'part time') members. They meet regularly, and make decisions on important policy issues. Members consist of the Party bosses of each of China's regions, heads of the main state-owned enterprises (SOEs), some army figures, and also government ministers. From this number the Politburo is elected. This has twenty-five members. Above this, at the summit of decision-making, is the Standing Committee of the Politburo, which currently has only nine members. The leaders of China are all members of the Standing Committee, and include the current president, Hu Jintao, and the current premier, Wen Jiabao.

Every single province of China has a Party secretary and two deputies. They are there to ensure that the Communist Party central policy is not being violated and that the 'political direction' of China, across its vastly contrasting different areas, is consistent. Every five years the CCP holds a major meeting, the Party Congress. The last of these was held in 2007; the next will be in 2012. They make decisions on the next five years of Party policy, and also elect members of the Politburo. In 2012, both Premier Wen and President and National Party Secretary Hu Jintao will step down. The Party Congress in this year will therefore be responsible for electing two new leaders. They will then be in power for the next five years, with the option to extend for another five years. Retirement age for senior Party positions is currently set at 67 years.

China's military, the PLA (which includes China's air force and navy), is controlled by a Party committee called the Central Military Commission (CMC), which is currently chaired by the CCP head, Hu Jintao. This shows that in China the military answers to the CCP – not to the government, or to anyone else. There is no separation of powers as there is in, for instance, the UK. Other sensitive areas, such as security, intelligence and policing, also take their instructions from committees under the CCP, not from the government.

THE GOVERNMENT

The Chinese government is in charge of the day-to-day running of the country. It has twenty-nine ministries, ranging from education to railways, information and trade. The number has been reduced from forty-three ministries in the 1990s. There are over 30 million civil servants, with many ministries having branch offices in China's provinces. Two of the most powerful ministries are the National Development and Reform Commission (NDRC), which is in charge of economic planning, and the Ministry of Finance, which is similar to the Treasury in the UK and the USA. Of these twenty-nine ministries, the leaders of all but two are currently Party members.

Government in China is coordinated through the State Council. This body is chaired by the premier and head of government, Wen Jiabao, and acts like the Cabinet Office in the UK or the Office of the President in the USA. It is in charge of coordinating the ministries, and dealing with major areas of shared policy. It has responsibility, for instance, for energy policy. It is also responsible for the Five Year Plans, for the main budgets that are issued, the current one of which runs from 2011 to 2015, and sets targets for economic growth, industrial policy, energy and the environment. It also issues, through its Information Office, key policy documents on medium- to long-term objectives.

In every province in China there are governors, who work along-side the Party secretaries and are responsible for the administration of their areas. Each has as many as seven or eight deputies. This structure continues down to the prefectures, districts and towns, where there are mayors and deputy mayors.

There is no clear regulation setting out where the responsibilities of the government and those of the Party begin and end. This is one of the most confusing things about the PRC. One can best understand the relationship between the two as being like that between whichever political party is in power in the UK and the civil service and machinery of government that carry out the ruling party's manifesto and are responsible for implementing it.

PEOPLE'S CONGRESSES

In addition to the CCP and the government are the People's Congresses. According to China's constitution, these are the key decision-making bodies in China, through which the people are able to express their will and to whom the CCP and the government are answerable. In fact, things are a little more complicated than this. There are five levels of congress, from those representing townships with populations of a few million up to those representing the whole country. The National People's Congress (NPC) is called China's parliament, and has almost 3,000 members. It meets for two to three weeks, usually in the spring, once a year. It differs from the British Parliament, however, in a number of important respects. There are no universal elections for its members, who are instead appointed by local governments from local congresses. They are meant to represent a cross section of interests in society. So there are a set number from China's fifty-six recognised ethnic groups, and members representing businesses, specific regions, the trade union (which is government-run) and other special interest groups. Congress members do not, therefore, represent specific constituencies like they do in the UK or USA. And their powers of initiating or changing laws are very limited. They work alongside the Chinese People's Political Consultative Conference (CCPPC), which again has a national membership of about 3,000 people, and acts as an advisory body. Like the Congress (the two usually meet at the same time and are called the 'two meetings') members do not have to belong to the CCP.

People's Congresses are seen as giving the Chinese public some say in lawmaking, governance and other important issues. The National People's Congresses are meant to discuss and then pass laws that are put before them.

THE COURTS AND OTHER GROUPS

Most people inside and outside China agree that under Mao Zedong, from 1949 to 1976, China had what is called 'rule of man', and that since 1978 it has been establishing 'rule of law'. Under Mao, huge powers were concentrated in the hands of one man. He acted like an all-powerful emperor, and was accountable to no laws. In the last three decades China has set up a legal system and trained many hundreds of thousands of lawyers, creating laws, many of them from scratch. China has courts at provincial and national levels, and a Supreme Court, whose head sits on the State Council.

Despite the big steps forward in introducing proper courts and a legal system, there is widespread agreement that Chinese judges would never be able to challenge the CCP and overrule any of its decisions. Whereas, therefore, in the UK and the USA the courts often issue decisions against the government, in China at the moment this would be unthinkable.

In addition to the courts, there are also a huge number of civil society groups – or NGOs – ranging from those representing business to environmental groups, special interest groups, and so on. These have no formal power, but they do have influence, and can lobby the government to make changes to laws.

WHERE THE REAL POWER IS

Of all of these groups for the organisation and guiding of society, the CCP is, in the end, by far the most powerful. It has control over the key positions in the People's Congresses, the government ministries and the courts. None of these is able to challenge the Party's power. China does have a constitution, which is meant to guarantee everyone's rights. Its very first articles state that China is a country where the people are the masters, and the Communist Party is the organisation that defends people's rights, and takes the leadership over all key matters. Those who challenge the Communist Party's right, like dissidents or pressure groups, are often put under a great deal of pressure. Some individuals have been jailed, and others made to leave the country.

The Communist Party says that it defends and protects people in two ways. These are its continuing source of power in China. The first is that the Communists restored China to unity after many decades of being weak, exploited by others and unstable. This was discussed earlier. The CCP says that it has made China a stable, unified country. The second way is the economic benefits the Party has delivered in the last thirty years. In 1949, because of war, China had barely any infrastructure, and most of its factories and railways had been destroyed. It was a country where the average age was only 35, and where over 90 per cent of the people lived in the countryside. In the last six decades, the CCP has ruled over a country that in 2010 was the world's second largest economy; rebuilt its trains, roads and airport infrastructure; lifted many hundreds of millions out of poverty; and become one of the economic powerhouses of the world. The CCP argues that without its unified, strong leadership none of this would have been possible. It also argues that events like the Great Leap Forward, in which many millions died of starvation in the 1960s, the Cultural Revolution, in which some areas of China were reduced to chaos, and the 1989 student demonstrations were all challenges along a path which the CCP, all said and done, is leading China to a better, brighter future.

2

Democracy... with Chinese characteristics

'Democracy', despite common misperceptions, is not a taboo word in China. Leaders in the PRC from Mao Zedong onwards have used the word frequently and discussed its meaning. The current president and Party secretary, Hu Jintao, in one of his most import speeches, at the major Party Congress in October 2007, used the word *minzhu*, which is the Chinese for 'democracy', more than sixty times in the space of two hours. Talking of 'putting people first', one of the key mantras of the current leadership, he promised to 'expand socialist democracy', and to do this through allowing 'Chinese citizens to participate in political affairs'. Primary-level democracy (meaning at the lower levels of government) would be improved. And within the Party, he said, there was increasing need to implement 'intra Party democracy.'[1]

Such claims sit somewhat oddly with a government that at the same time is able to dispatch one of the main authors of the pro-democracy public letter Charter 08 to jail in December 2009. Liu Xiaobo stated in this document, signed by more than 2,000 citizens:

> the Chinese government's approach to 'modernization' has proven disastrous. It has stripped people of their rights, destroyed their dignity, and corrupted normal human intercourse. So we ask:

Where is China headed in the twenty-first century? Will it continue with 'modernization' under authoritarian rule, or will it embrace universal human values, join the mainstream of civilized nations, and build a democratic system? There can be no avoiding these questions.[2]

For Liu and his co-signatories, democracy has four aspects:

(1) Political power begins with the people and the legitimacy of a regime derives from the people; (2) Political power is exercised through choices that the people make; (3) The holders of major official posts in government at all levels are determined through periodic competitive elections; (4) While honouring the will of the majority, the fundamental dignity, freedom and human rights of minorities are protected.

Their list of suggestions includes the need for the election of public officials, the separation of powers, independent courts, and a properly elected legislature.

No official with significant resource allocation powers is elected by any form of universal suffrage at the moment. Village elections, as will be seen later, only take place for the most local officials, with very limited powers and resources. Although most of Liu's suggestions have been discussed openly and unproblematically in China for some time, they were regarded as incendiary enough for him to be sent to jail for eleven years. He was awarded the Nobel Peace Prize in 2010.

The division between the two positions of Charter 08 and Hu Jintao's speech shows just how contentious the simple word 'democracy' is in the current PRC. It has become one of the key battlegrounds. Hu Jintao can call democracy 'the common pursuit of mankind'.[3] Wen Jiabao, the premier, can say that 'developing democracy and improving the legal system are basic requirements on the socialist system.'[4] But once one moves into the detail of what kind of democracy, and how it is implemented, structured and developed, arguments start. 'Democracy', political scientist

John Keane writes, 'has become one of those English words, like "computer" and "ok", familiar to millions of people around the world.'[5] But the idea that democracy can be a universal panacea for all global ills is not a helpful one. Keane himself refers to the conflict between participatory democracy (where means are found for people to express a view directly on issues relating to them) and representative democracy (where people are elected who then make decisions on behalf of those who elected them) – but for each different form that democracy takes, there is the issue of how best to engage the public in a process which in the end is neither over-onerous, nor ends up with elites (even elected ones) making decisions that are opposed by most in the society they are meant to represent. Only one country, for instance, in the 27-country-strong European Union allowed a public vote for the Lisbon Treaty in 2009 (Ireland). The rest passed it through highly managed parliamentary votes.

Socialism is great, but democracy is good

In China, it is permissible to say that 'democracy is a good thing'. One party official, Yu Keping, has written a whole essay on the subject with this very title, which has been widely circulated in Chinese within the PRC. In stark contrast to Liu Xiaobo, he continues to enjoy freedom and has maintained his position as the deputy director of the Translation and Compilation Bureau of the Communist Party Central Committee (CPCC). 'Democracy is a good thing', he argues, because it curtails the powers of officials who might use them for private gain. With corruption a major problem, this is obviously a big attraction. However, Yu continues, 'just because democracy is a good thing, that does not mean that everything about democracy is good.' It can sometimes 'allow sweet talking politicians to mislead the public'.[6] Democracy comes with a price, it comes with conditions, and it comes with risks. The risks are the thing that the CCP most dislikes about democracy.

Chinese leaders are willing to talk about 'democracy', but they define it in their own terms. What might those terms be? They have admitted that there are a range of issues that they need to deal with in the governance of their vast and complex country. There is increasing inequality. From 2004 to 2008 alone there were 12 million petitions to the central government because people were angry and frustrated with the way that local officials were dealing with issues like tax, land rights and compensation for accidents. Yu Jianrong, an academic at the Chinese Academy of Social Science and an adviser to the government, spoke in December 2009 – a day after dissident Liu Xiaobo had been sentenced – of China being beset by 90,000 cases of mass unrest a year in the previous three years. He divides these incidents into those classified as 'standing up for legal rights' (*weiquan*), 'venting air' (*xipeng*) incidents (where security offices have mishandled a situation, resulting in large public protests), and 'chaotic incidents' (*saoluan*) caused by exploitation of the breakdown of social stability in some areas by lawless elements. 'There is a view which has been held for a long time that Chinese society will experience large social disturbance. This year at least [2009], that notion has become more discussed, and more commonly held.'[7]

It is true that since China's entry to the World Trade Organization (WTO) in 2001, after fourteen years of negotiation, economic growth has exploded. In the space of merely ten years, China has become the world's second largest economy, the largest exporter, the holder of the largest amount of foreign reserves, and the second most popular inward investment destination after the USA. Such rapid growth has had a disorientating effect on society. Guobin Yang has stated that the current period has been one of contention. 'There were 8,700 mass incidents in 1993', he writes in a book about online activism in China.

> This number rose to 32,000 in 1999, 58,000 in 2003, and 87,000 in 2005.[8] Accompanying the alarming ascendance of social conflicts in recent years is the appearance of an official rhetoric of building a 'harmonious society.' Perhaps more than anything else, this new

discourse indicates that Chinese society has entered an age of contention.[9]

In order to achieve a 'harmonious society', as President Hu and Premier Wen continue to stress, there is a need to encourage systems, processes and structures in society that help stability, and deal with some of these conflicts and sources of contention. The rule of law is one area where they have expended a lot of effort. Civil society groups have emerged in many different areas, dealing with issues ranging from the environment to migrant workers, to the rights of ethnic minorities, to public participation in decision-making. All of these have a link to political reform, and to democratisation.

'The Six Whys'

Talk of Western models is something the CCP resists. In a book published in June 2009, via the official newspaper of the Chinese government, the *People's Daily*, six areas where there had been discussion and demand were set out. Called 'The Six Whys' (see box) the second and fifth deal most directly with suggestions that China needs to copy Western liberal democracies. The authors argue that Marxism is scientific and a source of progress. It is not just 'of economic use but is objective truth'. Stating somewhat paradoxically that 'Western ideologies such as liberalism, social Darwinism, anarchism, realism ... are all unable to resolve China's problems',[10] Marxism (which to many might also rank as a foreign import) is given a 'leading role' in society, allowing spaces for other ideas.[11] Ideological pluralism would create instability. The global economic crisis from 2008 onwards is cited as a proof that imposing Western values on China would be dangerous and destabilising.[12] 'At the moment', the authors state,

> we are living in a period of great development and change, where there are profound international and internal changes happening in the situation, and the ideological struggle is becoming much fiercer,

The Six Whys

1. Why we must resolutely persist in placing Marxism in a leadership position in the ideological realm, and not introduce pluralism.

2. Why it is that only with socialism can we save China, only with socialism with Chinese characteristics can we develop China, and not with democratic socialism and capitalism.

3. Why we must resolutely persist with the structure of the People's Congresses, and not introduce 'the tripartite division of powers'.

4. Why we must persist with the united front under the CCP, and not have a Western-style multiparty system.

5. Why we must persist with public ownership as the base, with a mixed economy, and not have privatisation.

6. Why we must persist with opening up and reform, and not return to the past.

so we must not give up putting Marxism in the leading position ideologically.[13] This serves as a basis for social stability, and a bulwark against chaos.

The economic success of the 'Reform and Opening Up' process since 1978 has given the CCP a new legitimacy.[14] Even the model of Western democratic socialism is therefore not relevant to this local task, because it has 'become the companion to capitalism'.[15] As the 1982 Chinese constitution states in its second article, in 'The People's Republic of China ... all power belongs to the people.'[16] The people are represented through the various levels of the People's Congress, from country, to prefectural, to provincial, and then national levels. The National People's Congress (NPC) is 'the basis of political life in China'.[17] Having a separation of power into legal, administrative and legislative realms, on the Western model, would create destabilising divisions, introduce new class and power conflicts and go against the sovereignty of the NPC.[18] There is no common political model that can be used everywhere in the world, the authors state, and the NPC system suits China's specific characteristics. The NPC works 'under the leadership of the CCP'. In such a structure, there is no need for multiple parties. The authors claim that these would be a source of instability.[19] Parties as they exist in Europe and the United States 'are a product of the particular system of capitalism and capitalist interests dominant there'.[20] The CCP is able to gather all the different viewpoints into a united front, hearing their views through consultative bodies. This is the best way to serve the 'common interest'.[21]

'The Six Whys' could just as well be called 'The Six Nos'. At the heart of the defensiveness of the CCP towards any attempts to introduce reforms is the position of the CCP itself. Put bluntly, while the CCP is happy to introduce moves to make some areas of government accountable and transparent, and has even introduced an Open Government Information rule in 2008, which gives citizens similar powers to demand to see official information that they have in Europe or North America, opening up the deepest recesses of the CCP and its inner working to the outside world is not going to happen any time soon. Perhaps as a sign of this, even 'The Six Whys', with its highly conventional and conservative formulations, was met with silent anger among the more reformist elements in the Party, and with irritation for not going further by the harder elements.

Debating democracy at the Party School

Much of the intense debate about democracy and its future in China is carried out in the Party School network. For those who say that ideology is no longer important in China, and that the CCP has jettisoned its historic interest in theorising on the nature of society, the Party Schools, of which there are some 2,000 across the country, are an unfortunate aberration. That the CCP puts so much effort, time and resources into training its key officials (more commonly known as cadres) must prove that ideological issues are still important. And while the CCP cooperates and works with a market economy and some elements of capitalism, at its heart it is not reconciled, and cedes ground slowly and grudgingly. Marketisation has delivered economic growth, and that has delivered stability for the CCP. But that doesn't stop CCP elite leaders talking about them creating 'the primary stage of socialism' rather than being on a process towards a free-market, Western-style economy and political system. Party Schools offer the cadres being trained in them what academic Frank Pieke has described as 'a combination of advanced knowledge, ideological discipline, normative and moral guidance and access to the power, wishes, and desires of the leadership'.[22] They are regarded by many experts on China as the place for some of the freest, boldest thinking in China today.

The Central Party School in Beijing is out in the north-east of the city close to the prestigious Qinghua and Beijing university campuses, and on the bus route to the Summer Palace. As with most places of any importance in the running of modern China, there are no large signs declaring that this is the Central Party School. A long driveway leads to a reception office beside a gate. Inside the institution has the feel of an old-style office block or teaching area of a university, the type that was built throughout the country from the 1950s into the early 1980s. It is not the sort of place simply to show up hoping for a meeting. Access is difficult, and to speak there an honour bestowed only on the likes of Jacques Derrida, who baffled the assembled teachers and students in 2001, Jürgen Habermas, and politicians like Peter Mandelson. As a clear indication of its prestige, the two most recent school presidents have been Hu Jintao and Xi Jinping, both of them members of the Politburo, and one of them the country's president. Xi is the man most likely to succeed Hu in the coming leadership change in 2012.

In 2007 three academics from the Party School published a book titled *Storming the Fortress* (*Gong Jian*), which offered a blueprint for China's political reform following on from the NPC which had just been held. The book became something of a blockbuster.[23] Quoting Hu Jintao the authors declare that 'with no democracy there is no socialism'.[24] Faced with the continuing problems of sustainable economic development, agricultural and rural reform, social security and stability, and the challenges of the environment, China 'needs a strong [*qiangli*] political system. Without this, we cannot resolve these problems.'[25] Staying within the broad parameters set by Hu, *Storming the Fortress* divides its blueprint for China's political reform into four broad areas: the rule of law; the training and education of cadres; the management of news and information; and intra-Party democracy. But at the very beginning, and indeed throughout their various discussions, they clarify one critical piece of ideological certainty: 'Without the leadership of the CPC, there will be no progress in the reform of China's political system, and the development of China as a nation has no future.'[26] Democratic accountability exists, and will be strengthened, by the People's Congresses at their various local, provincial and national levels. But while 'in terms of law the Congresses are the highest state organs ... in the political life of China they come under the leadership of the Party.'[27] A similar thing is said about courts, and about civil society groups, all of which have their crucial functions recognised, but all of which have to come under the political direction of the CCP. This is a crucial issue. The CCP's authority and leadership function in society cannot be challenged. While it is therefore acceptable to storm the fortress of society, it is not acceptable to direct any of this at the CCP. That remains a protected, carefully policed territory.

Speaking to one of the authors in Beijing in the summer of 2009, I was struck by how deeply their study of what had happened in the Soviet Union and other countries that had experienced a 'colour revolution' has shaped their current thinking. In their eyes the fall of the USSR was not a good thing. It pushed Russia into economic decline, which it took a decade to reverse. Its most tragic impact was in reducing the life expectancy of men from the early sixties down to the mid-fifties in the space of a few years. This had a devastating impact on society. Alcoholism and ill health became rife. These are not attractive adverts for China to look at in order to figure out its own future reform. But the author was adamant that the greatest issue that needed facing in China was how to create consensus. And at the moment the CCP was the best means of delivering this. Across all of the different, often competing, sometimes conflicting groups in society that have arisen in the last three decades of economic reform, how is an efficient, sustainable and stable form of participatory governance achievable?

The current answer to this is simply through greater democracy within the CCP. There is no dispute within the CCP, therefore, about democracy being a good thing. But some forms of democracy have created instability, unsustainability and impeded economic growth, which is seen as being deeply undesirable for China's current stage of development. Or, as Hu put it in his 2007 speech:

> At present and for a period to come, the Communist Party of China and the Chinese government will actively and steadily push forward the reform of the political system, stick to and improve the socialist democratic system, strengthen and improve the socialist legal system, reform and improve the methods of leadership and rule of the CPC, reform and improve the government's decision-making mechanism, promote the reform of the system of administrative management, boost the reform of the judicial system, deepen the reform of the cadre and personnel system, reinforce the restraint and supervision over power, strive to maintain social stability, and promote economic development and social progress in an all-round way.

That means no universal suffrage, no organised political opposition, and no Western-style parliaments with representative democracy – for the moment. I will return to the specifics of the Party School vision of political change in society in the final chapter.

The White Paper on Democracy

In 2005, the central government, through the state information office, issued a White Paper titled 'Building of Political Democracy in China'. The paper states:

Since China adopted the reform and opening up policies at the end of the 1970s, while making efforts to steadily deepen the reforms of its economic system, the country has unswervingly pushed forward reforms of its political system. China's democratic system has been continuously improved and the forms of democracy are becoming more varied. The people are exercising fully their right to be masters of the state. The building of political democracy with Chinese characteristics is progressing with the times, exhibiting great vigour and vitality.[28]

After spelling out the unique historical conditions and traditions of China, called by the paper's author's 'a long history of feudal society', the document speaks of the CCP delivering New Democracy 'characterised by thorough opposition to imperialism, feudalism and bureaucratic capitalism'. In this context, Chinese democracy had come into being. What is it? It is, according to the document, 'a people's democracy under the leadership of the CCP... The Chinese people won the right to be masters of the state only after many years of arduous struggle under the leadership of the CCP.' The Communist Party is critical. Its leadership 'is a fundamental guarantee for the Chinese people to be masters in managing the affairs of their own country'. Such a democracy is one where 'the overwhelming majority of the people act as masters of state affairs'. It is one which is 'guaranteed by the people's democratic dictatorship', and where 'democratic centralism' is 'the basis organisation principle and mode of operation'.

The White Paper works through the key functional attributes of the current Chinese system – the Party in a leadership role, the People's Congress system, multiparty cooperation and political consultation through the Chinese Consultative People's Political Conference (CCPPC), ethnic regional autonomy, and 'grassroots democracy in urban and rural areas'. 'Self-government by villagers', the paper states, 'is a basic system by which the broad masses of the rural people directly exercise their democratic rights to run their own affairs'. With 800 million of China's 1.3 billion population still classified as rural residents (though as many as 200 million belong to the floating population, and therefore largely live in urbanised areas), a means of enfranchising this vast portion of the population is needed. The reasons behind this will be looked at later, along with the mechanisms by which, in effect, this has been done. But the White Paper makes clear that self-government for villages is a key part of the governance structure of modern China. Village Committees are the main entities by which this is carried out, composed of three to seven members, including the chair and vice chair, and serving for three years. 'The villagers are enthusiastic about these elections and, according to incomplete statistics, the average participation in such elections is above 80 per cent.' They deliver 'democratic decision-making, democratic management, and democratic supervision'. Parallel to this is the establishment of urban neighbourhood committees in cities, again 'to enable self-management, and to embed grassroots democracy in Chinese cities'.

The articulation of democratic rule in the White Paper is very specific, and heavily circumscribed. It means, in essence, the CCP sticking 'to the principle of ruling the country for the people and relying on the people in its rule'. It means 'reforming and improving the leadership system and working mechanism leadership of the state and society' through the 'political, ideological and organisational leadership' of the CCP. And, more recently, it means 'developing intra-Party democracy', which involves improving the Party congress system, giving a greater role to Party committees, and doing something about the supervision of cadres and intra-Party entities (a huge numbers of officials were punished in various ways, up to and including the death sentence, for corruption in 2008 and 2009; 130,000 were punished in 2009 alone).

The White Paper sets out five benchmarks for the future: (1) Maintaining the unity and leadership of the CCP; (2) Maintaining socialism; (3) Supporting social stability; (4) Safeguarding sovereignty; (5) Being 'in accord with the objective law of progress'.

It asserts that 'A complete model of democracy cannot be built overnight.'

Same old same old

Those with long enough memories may well find on reading the 2007 White Paper that certain phrases, and indeed whole chunks of the document, fill them with a powerful sense of déjà vu. A look at one of the earliest studies of Chinese communist ideology from 1963, almost half a century before, will prove why. American scholar John Wilson Lewis wrote in that year that

> leadership in Marxist–Leninist theory is not a matter of power but of correct relationship. The working masses are in principle as-sumed to hold all power. The party, as the vanguard of the working class, exercises leadership as its principal function in the mass line process.[29]

Quoting an early ideologue, Lewis notes that 'Without the Communist Party, there is no New China',[30] continuing that 'the mass of the people look upon them [party members] as their dearest closest friends...'[31] The masses 'are the creators of history'. The Party, according to one of the founding fathers of the PRC, and president of the country until 1966, Liu Shaoqi, and quoted by Lewis, 'must represent the interests of the masses'. To maintain the correct line, 'from the masses to the masses', it is necessary 'to establish close contact "not only between the Party and the masses outside the Party (the class and the people) but first of all between the leading bodies of the Party and the masses within the Party (the cadres and the membership)".'[32] A further quotation states that

> democracy ... is manifested in the constitutional rights of the people..., the cadres' meetings and the unity of cadres and masses, the autonomous regions, the policy toward democratic parties of 'long term co-existence and mutual supervision'.[33]

If we replace 'masses' and 'working class' simply with 'people', the quotations above could easily be from today. There has, of course, been a development and evolution of CCP ideology and thought. Class struggle has been abandoned. A free market has been accepted. Utopianism lingers, but is less explicit than it was under the more idealistic Maoist period. But the central tenet remains: that the CCP is central to China's political life, and to the leadership of the people. So all of the language in the White Paper, and all other official discourse of democratisation in China, is built around this. Anything that abnegates and denies that tenet is in danger of falling into outlawed language, with the punishment that entails.

Other voices: consultative democracy

There has been a lively debate about the nature of democracy within the parameters set out by the official discourse and position, best represented by the 2007 White Paper. Pan Wei, at Beijing University, produced one such formulation in 2004 when he spoke of 'consultative rule of law'. 'Chinese leaders are not ready to go anywhere, but they know they need to go somewhere', he says. Stasis for the medium to long term is not adequate. But to present democracy as a solution to all the CCP's ills is wrong in Pan's view. 'The mythologizing definition of democracy often implies the function of a panacea.'[34] Often, 'democracy appears more like an ideology.'[35] The rule of law, however, is a different issue: 'Democracy and rule of law differ in basic approaches... Rule of law is to regulate a government instead of creating a government.'[36] And while democracy needs what Pan calls the 'four freedoms' – of press, speech, assembly and association – it cannot guarantee these; only the law can do that.[37] In order to face down corruption (one of the PRC's greatest current problems), democracy is far less effective than the rule of law, which would provide a standard and series of rules to prevent officials using their positions for private gain.[38] Democracy without the rule of law is meaningless, offering 'a tendency of self-destruction, leading to an easy decay from democracy to autocracy'.[39] Pan accepts up to a point the elite view that China's specific conditions mean it needs a unique form of democracy – 'neither a pure democracy nor a democracy supplemented by rule of law, but rule of law supplemented by democracy'.[40] To justify this, Pan refers to Chinese history with, he claims, its tradition of economic liberty and absence of the elite-dominated power structures that existed in the West. This is highly contentious, but his end point perhaps has more traction, referring to the unique complexity of Chinese society as it exists now. The fear of factionalism exploiting these fractures within Chinese society and creating instability, because this sort of disunity has existed in living memory, is very real. Instead, 'partisan politics … has no natural legitimacy in the Chinese tradition.'[41] This serves to legitimise the Communist Party's disallowance of multiparty competition. The most appropriate political model for China to adopt therefore, what Pan calls the 'consultative rule of law', would take into account its challenges of accountability for rulers, creating social consensus and providing stable rule.

In order to do this the political elite would need to undertake a profound change of direction, from their current emphasis focusing on economic development to creating instead the rule of law as their key priority.[42] This would entail a number of institutional changes: the dividing line between government and the Party would need to be clarified constitutionally and in political practice; there would need to be a much more robust organisational treatment of corruption, with the Party ceding some of its self-regulatory powers to a genuine outside body; and somehow a means would need to be found of dealing with the division between officials and the legal system, to prevent political interference in the judicial process. None of that entails what Pan calls a mass conversion to Western-style liberal democracy, to which he imputes many faults and problems. But it would head off some of the larger challenges facing the Chinese body politic in the years ahead.

China's political option in the future could be so unique that it might again surprise the world. China has surprised the world with a unique traditional polity, with the Communist takeover, with the Cultural Revolution, with the result of Tiananmen, and with a huge economic miracle amid the economic collapse of nearly all the other formerly communist countries... That may be just another surprise to come.[43]

Pan's message for the elites is as double-edged as that of the more populist commentators. While not daring to confront the CCP's monopoly on power, he does recognise that the focus on economic growth pure and simple is a game with diminishing returns, now that China has met many of its performance benchmarks and is well on the way to constructing a 'moderately well off middle income country'. From now on, as the explosion of civil society, non-state businesses, website groups and other indicators show, the aspirations of many segments of China's complex population become much more varied and complicated. It is no longer just about filling people's stomachs, if it ever was. Shifting to a political programme that is a little more nuanced, like constructing the rule of law, while avoiding multiparty politics, might offer a future programme the CCP could feel comfortable with. This is regardless of some of the very sweeping generalisations Pan makes about the cultural appropriateness of democracy within China, comments which critics of his proposal say support the ingrained belief in paternalistic, elite-led government and administration in China historically, and in the PRC to this day. Perhaps this paternalistic, hierarchical structure should become the real target for change, because whatever evidence there is shows that this sort of moral standing imputed to officials is, in fact, something that all too many of them have shown themselves unworthy of.

Many voices, one problem

The perspectives above offer current views, from different points, on the condition of China's current political state, and also on where there might be changes. The voice of the elite, through 'The

Six Whys', is a defence of the status quo, asserting that the PRC's overarching system, ideologically and administratively, is fit for purpose, and that the key issue is to persist with it and not to deviate to inappropriate imported and potentially corrupting models. For Pan Wei, and for the authors of *Storming the Fortress*, there is a recognition (largely, it has to be admitted, absent from 'The Six Whys') of the need for profound change, but in administrative areas, and in deepening the rule of law and the role and function of consultation and the bodies this is done through. Only with Liu Xiaobo and Charter 08 is there a direct confrontation with the role of the CCP, with its monopoly on power perceived as the key issue that needs to be addressed. Unsurprisingly, his voice has been silenced in debate in mainland China.

In fact, the distinctive role of the Party in what some analysts have called the 'Party State' is the biggest issue that overshadows all of these separate discussions. This is a striking characteristic. It is clear, in major policy declarations by the elite leadership of the CCP and in their actions, that they do not contemplate surrendering their monopoly on power any time soon, whatever compromises they might be making to deliver greater legitimacy to their rule through wider consultation, deeper rule-of-law reform, and other innovations. 'The Six Whys' is striking in its assertion of the primacy of the CCP and its ideological and administrative mode of operating. This has been cleverly harnessed to the sense of a specifically 'Chinese' way of governing to which this model is particularly appropriate. Again, there are searching questions about just how predetermined and inevitable this unitary system has been and is for the Chinese.

Storming the Fortress offers at least some practical steps to deal with the key challenges of how to deliver consensus for decisions across society, especially in a time of increasing dislocation and contention, and how to regulate and discipline the roles of officials. For these authors, this has to come through greater transparency, greater independent scrutiny, and deeper consultation with bodies that have meaningful powers to hold those governing China to account. There is a strong awareness across the voices of disaffection considered above of the corrosive impact of corruption on the moral and practical standing of officials in China. Pan Wei speaks of the fact that 'it is widely believed within the Communist Party that if the regime falls, corruption will be the most immediate cause.'[44] Hu Jintao and Wen Jiabao have made combating corruption one of their key objectives, even allowing fellow members of the Politburo like former Party secretary of Shanghai Chen Liangyu to be felled in 2006 by allegations of misappropriation of public funds.[45] Chen was subsequently found guilty and sentenced in 2007 to sixteen years in prison, and is currently serving out his sentence.[46]

But how meaningful are anti-corruption measures when the CCP remains largely opaque to those who are not within its elite circles? The authors of *Storming the Fortress* speak about the congresses and courts delivering greater scrutiny to budgets, and decision-making processes, and holding officials to the law. Yet there is no discussion, even in their terms, of this also happening within the Party. If, as most believe, the CCP is the real power holder in China, then accountability within itself is most important. But any moves to provide this, even with the current 'intra-Party democracy' promoted by Hu Jintao, have to accept the proposition that the Party can be both its own rule-maker and its own policeman. Any discussion of how possible this is, and of how the position should be remedied by genuine entities outside the CCP that can hold the Party to account, are still categorised as dissident, subversive and hence outlawed in PRC discourse about political and administrative reform. This might strike some onlookers as akin to allowing banks that had flagrantly exploited and abused the liberal financial environment before the economic crisis and collapse of 2008 to continue with business as usual by accepting their argument that they are in the best position to regulate their own affairs. In effect, therefore, the most fundamental issue in contemporary Chinese political life – the accountability and subjection to the rule of law of the CCP itself

– remains outside the bounds of permissible discussion. A number of 'firewalls' have been created to deepen the outlawing of this whole area of possible discourse, from the blaming of such processes for leading to the collapse of governance, and then economies, after the colour revolutions in the former Soviet Union and its satellites, to imposing a culturalist notion that such attempts are 'unChinese' and therefore a foreign plot to weaken and undermine the PRC and bring back disunity.

With so much power, however, it is hard to see how the CCP can prevent this whole discourse of political reform creeping closer, to the point where there is increasing recognition that it, and not other administrative or social or geopolitical areas, is the main problem, and that it needs to reform itself radically. How a monolithic, self-regulating system can do this remains the big question. Is it possible for a unified CCP to introduce the things it says it needs for stable and efficient governance, like greater rule of law, better scrutiny over budgets, enhanced access to free information, fuller participation by the public in decision-making, without finally creating the space in which a genuine political opponent and challenger to its rule appears? On the CCP's own reckoning, civil society and the legal system have become just such a challenge in other former communist countries. How can the CCP stop this?

For all the continuing repression within the PRC in the late Hu-Wen era, therefore, it is clear that the space for legitimate discussion of political options, and the need for fundamental change, is growing. The moment is gradually approaching when there will be open talk of a future in which the CCP is itself forced to undergo profound changes in the way it accounts for its powers, its role in society, its own internal governance, and its exercise of power. The voices quoted above, beyond that of the elite, are all contributions to this immense debate. But village elections are the one area where one can say that real measures have been taken that look and feel like the way democracy is practised in the West. It is to these that we now turn to hear what the non-elite Chinese people think.

The structure of administration in China[47]

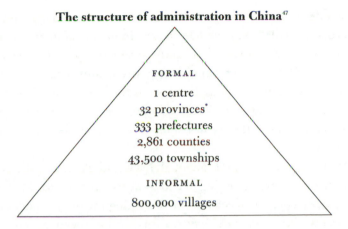

FORMAL

1 centre
32 provinces*
333 prefectures
2,861 counties
43,500 townships

INFORMAL

800,000 villages

* This figure includes 4 municipalities directly under the central government, 5 autonomous regions and Taiwan, which Mainland China still regards as part of its own sovereign territory.

When things go wrong: village elections creating contention[48]

At the heart of the big story of Chinese rural democracy are the many millions of smaller stories of those who have been touched by this immense process. Before looking at village elections, therefore, here is one story, of one man, who tried to stand in a village election, and of what happened to him. It is such concrete experiences of engaging in the whole process of rural democracy that give village democracy its tremendous significance and interest.

Mr Wang Jinsheng is 55, a native of a rural area of the impoverished western province of Shanxi. Shanxi may well be the home of the Terracotta Warriors, near to the main city of Xian, and boast a splendid history dating back thousands of years, culminating in its time as the capital of what was then China during the mighty Tang dynasty from the seventh to the tenth centuries, but it now exists as a place with its best days behind it. While the rest of China hurtles ahead towards some kind of über-modernity, Shanxi suffers from a degraded environment, lack of infrastructure, a state-owned enterprise sector dominated by heavy industry, and, in some of the more isolated areas, deep and entrenched poverty. Even so, because of China's burgeoning energy needs and reliance on coal, with which the region is well endowed, those in its mining sector have in the last few years made a killing. Shanxi is today a poor province that nevertheless has some of the wealthiest individuals in the country.

Mr Wang is one of these, although his wealth is on a smaller scale than that of many. According to a local newspaper report, Mr Wang had been a 'common mechanic' before taking the opportunity to set up his own business in the 1980s, at the start of the great economic liberalisation process. He is now an energy and mining company president, but someone who has not forgotten his poor background, and who decided, fatefully, to put himself forward in his local village election. It was a decision that was to change his life. His case is typical of many among the new elites, especially business people, who are starting to want something more than the right just to make a lot of money.

Mr Wang had been very supportive of charities and educational projects in the village in which he chose to stand. According to a reporter from the Xinhua news agency, the official news outlet of the Chinese government, he 'had never forgotten his fellow villagers'. At the end of every year, he had donated foodstuffs, and given everyone over 60 years old, the disabled and the poor, 100 Chinese yuan (US$16.4). 'Mr Wang, a rich man who does not consider himself rich, wants to let everyone grow rich with him.'[49]

Mr Wang had, however, started to harbour ambitions in a more political direction. A great part of this was due to the then Village Committee leader, Mr Zhao. Mr Zhao had, according to testimony put together by Mr Wang after the events that subsequently unfolded, used his position to abuse the one significant power that is still wielded by elected Village Committee heads – that of being able to disburse land and to approve building and commercial projects.

From 2000 to 2008, Mr Zhao had allowed a number of construction projects, including some in which he had a personal interest. This was expressly against national and local regulations, which forbid the conversion of agricultural land for residential or commercial use. With only a small proportion of China's land arable, and with a massive population to support, it has become a national priority to preserve what agriculturally usable land is left. But rapid and massive urbanisation and the huge boom in the price of housing have been too great a temptation, and in many places building sites continue to encroach relentlessly onto rice fields and growing plots. 'The land', as Mr Wang's main deposition to the authorities begins, 'is a farmer's destiny. If they lose their land, they lose the basic means of materially making a living.'

In 2006, Mr Zhao had signed a contract with a local construction company for a fifty-year lease, worth 1 million yuan (approximately US$100,000). Five years earlier, he had been the middleman in a development involving the construction of a driving school centre, again on a fifty-year lease, and selling parts of the site for commercial property. The same year he had allowed a hospital to build shops, a factory and other commercial property on what had been agricultural land, again on a fifty-year lease. In 2004, 12.4 mu (a mu is equivalent to about 0.66 hectares) had been transferred to some associates to be used for, among other things, an entertainment centre. A hotel had been built on other land at a cost of over 1 million yuan ($145,000). In all, over a seven-year period, 120 mu (about 85 hectares) had been built on illegally. The net result had been to make many people in the village poor, with only 200 yuan (US$29.3) a year compensation each. '80 per cent of the villagers', Wang's deposition states, 'have no growing land.' While Zhao's relatives and associates had grown rich, natives of the area where he had been elected as representative had become increasingly more impoverished.

For this reason, Wang, as a businessman, had decided to stand against Zhao in the election for Village Committee head scheduled for December 2008 as a non-Party candidate. As part of Wang's election campaign he had prepared a 'notice', issued to all residents eligible to vote in the village. 'I am Wang Jinsheng', it states, 'the President of Jinxing Company, originally a factory head… I have come to take part in the competition for the head of the Village Committee.' His appeal continues: 'If this village needs me, I will work for the villagers. If the villagers want me, I will sort things out realistically for them. If everyone wants me, I will openly speak to people. I have promised myself, I will be honest to people, I will work hard, and I will be self-disciplined.' Part of Wang's appeal was that he was not just another cadre, but a businessman who had made his own way for twenty years. It was on this basis that he had felt it legitimate to stand.

The chronology of what followed in December 2008 is a classic example of how elections have become the arena for play-offs of power between new and old forces at the most basic level of governance in modern China. Wang had made his intentions clear about standing for the Village Committee position in November. On 26 November, however, a notice had been posted by the local election committee stating that there were two 'strict rules' that had to be adhered to by all those who intended to be candidates. One was that they had to be Communist Party members. The other was that they could not be more that 48 years old. In fact, national and local laws allow all those between the ages of 18 and 60, regardless of gender, ethnicity, Party membership or status, to stand in village elections. The only reason why such regulations were issued was, according to Wang, 'to confuse and cheat locals' who did not properly understand them or their own rights. Part of Wang's motivation in his campaign, therefore, was to make sure people knew that the regulations issued by the local committee were simply not true.

So angry had Wang been, in fact, that on 30 November he set up a meeting with seventeen other villagers to discuss how to respond to this issuing of new, irregular rules. On 1 December, Wang went to the local Village Committee offices to discuss the issue with Zhao. 'When Zhao left the room', Wang writes, 'I turned over a note he had left on the office table. On this he had written 'If Wang Jinsheng really wants to stand and be a leader, then let the police, the law, and the local public security bureau collect information and evidence about him, and think of a way of detaining him.' After seeing this, Wang said to himself, 'I do nothing illegal, I am disciplined, and abide by the law, so what can I be done for?'

The next day, with the seventeen others, Wang set off to report the matter to the next level of government, at the township close by. But the encounter proved to be unpleasant. 'Are you Wang Jinsheng?' a township official called Hou had begun, 'I wanted to find you anyway. That notice you put around yesterday was illegal.' Wang replied, 'Mr Hou, I didn't put up anything illegal, it was a notice about my election promises.' This angered Hou, who slammed his hand on the table. 'I say it was illegal, so it's illegal. I am warning you, you need to take responsibility for the illegal things you are doing.' When Wang tried to intercede, Hou continued, 'I'm telling you. You are not to take part in the election. You have to withdraw. Even if you get a thousand votes, you're not going to be elected. And even if Zhao gets only one vote, he is still going to succeed.' 'I want to take part in the election because the local people support me', Wang said. 'You're not qualified', snapped Hou, 'you're not a Party member and you're over 48.' When Wang demanded to see where these two laws were written down, another man with Hou produced a local book of regulations stating adamantly they were in that. But when Wang asked to see them on the page with his own eyes, Hou had barked at him, 'I can't waste more of my time talking to you.' The next day local officials came to put pressure on Wang's younger brother, telling him to ask Wang to see reason and withdraw. They even offered inducements in the form of unspecified compensation.

Because Wang showed no sign of withdrawing from the election, things escalated on 12 December with a summons to the local procurator, Mr Zhang. 'Old Wang', Zhang said,

> you've been a business person for years. I've heard about all the good things you've done for villagers. They really support you. But you can't be the Village Committee head. You can carry on doing

really important, useful things, but not as an elected official. You're not a Communist Party member, and you're too old. Withdraw now. It is the best thing to do.

As they talked, the head of the local Public Security Bureau (PSB – the Chinese version of the local police) 'happened to come by and invited me to talk with him at his offices', writes Wang. Being drawn ominously closer to the security agents and their world, Wang maintained his line: 'I can't withdraw from the election. Villagers have great expectations of me. If I withdraw now, what will they think? How will they look at me?' The PSB boss put it crisply: 'Don't you understand? This job is Zhao's because he's the choice of the local government. If you compete against him, then you are opposing them. And they are the ones we have to listen to.'

Taken to another security officer's room, Wang was presented with a piece of paper, on which was written the accusation that he had 'destroyed the process of the elections and committed fraud'. Stunned, Wang asked on what grounds this accusation was being made, and why he should sign something that he did not believe was true. 'It is because you improperly took seventeen villagers for dinner to gain their votes', he was told. This was construed as election rigging. Magically, at this point his nemesis Zhao appeared, and told him that 'this matter is out of both of our hands'.

As it was already late at night, Wang simply left, tired with the business. On 13 December Wang took all the materials he had gathered about the irregular rules and the property dealings of Zhao to the provincial government. They simply told him that they would instruct the local township to investigate matters and get back to him. A follow-up meeting held by the township on 15 December issued a notice saying that 'Wang Jinsheng is not an eligible candidate, not because of his qualifications, but because he tried to buy votes by entertaining voters.'

On 16 December, Wang was detained. On his second day in the local prison the first round of the election was held. Of 1,359 who cast their votes, he received 623, Zhao 531. Because no candidate received more than half the total votes cast, a second round was held, on 18 December. On this occasion, of the 1,367 votes, Wang received 724 votes and Zhao 517. This was despite Wang's claim that Zhao had generously entertained more than thirty friends and relatives in the village. Despite the clear mandate, on 23 December Zhao was reappointed as the Village Committee head. The next day a group of villagers went to protest the vote at the next level of government, the provincial headquarters. A number of them returned to the local township government offices the next day, but were promptly detained along with Wang.

After ten days in prison, Wang was let out on 26 December. It had, according to him, been a thirty-day-long nightmare. 'I realised', he said, 'that whatever the situation, if you wanted to be the Village Committee head it had nothing to do with elections. It was all stitched up beforehand.' The words of a town official came back to him: 'Our local government here in the town is a formal part of the administrative structure in China, not like villages, which are outside of this. Village elections have no impact on what we do. We can let whomever we want take part in these elections. We are the ones with the power.'

Wang had gathered 700 signatures to support his original candidacy. But on his own admission he had been up against a powerful coalition of vested interests, from township officials to security officers, to other businesses. Six months later, in the middle of 2009, he was pursuing his case at central government level, but his lawyer admitted that 'this kind of case is too common. If you don't push it immediately, then it gets lost in thousands of others like it.'

Wang's case illustrates well where village elections put the old Party against emerging new figures. Wang had given generously, and contributed a large amount to the victims in the Sichuan earthquake in early 2008. He had used the local and national press in his campaign. In many areas people like Wang achieve a breakthrough, but in others it ends up with violence. Some parts of Shanxi have not been able to hold elections for over a decade because they end in chaos and physical fights. For each of China's more than 800,000 villages the case is different. What Wang's story does show is a society where new sources of wealth and new classes are sometimes coming up against the Party and pushing their demands more assertively. Someone as persistent as Mr Wang will not be easy to keep down for long. And he is just one of many thousands. Their contribution to China's future could be more significant than people currently believe.

3

The village election process

In Fuping, rural Hubei, elections are held every three years. Fuping is a typical Chinese village – poor, with weak infrastructure and poor human development indicators. It is a place on the road to nowhere. Even in the brash, modernising, bold new China, almost half the population live in places like this.

2008 happened to be an election year. The themes for those standing in this campaign were the need to have roads built properly in the village, and security – there had been a recent crime wave. It was on these issues that the candidates fought for public support. The election itself took place in a school. There were five candidates. The hall on the day of the hustings was full. Unlike in Western elections, candidates are not able to produce leaflets before the actual election; nor can they go around to people's houses, talking to them on their doorsteps. Their main pitch is for five to ten minutes at the public meeting held the night before the election, when they can set out their case.

Some of these meetings can be lively, while others descend into out-and-out violence as discussions grow heated and contentious issues get raised. In others there are bands playing, and a festival-like atmosphere prevails. Election debate in Fuping was even-handed and civil. Candidates in other hustings ripped into each other, disagreeing vehemently on certain issues. According to one informal analysis, of the 1 million elections held over the last two decades, maybe half have been conducted well, and half have been problematic.

To ensure the rules are kept, officials from the next echelons of government, the township and county levels, have to be present. There are sometimes foreign observers from organisations like the Carter Center or the Ford Foundation (though less so nowadays – the reasons for which are discussed below). Officials from central ministries, like the Ministry of Civil Affairs, who take the lead in dealing with the administration of local elections, and the Agriculture Ministry, sometimes also attend.

Village elections in China have followed a simple process. According to the regulations issued by the national Ministry of Civil Affairs, there are four ways to be a candidate: you can be nominated by ten or more villagers; you can nominate yourself; you can be nominated by the local branch of the Communist Party; or you can be put forward by the current Village Committee. Before election day, lists of candidates are posted publicly. Article 9 of the Village Committee Law is clear about who can stand:

> Any villager who has reached the age of 18 ... regardless of their
> ethnic status, race, sex, occupation, family background, religious
> beliefs, education, property status and length of residence, with the
> exception of persons who have been deprived of political rights in
> accordance with the law.

On election day itself the villagers receive instructions on how to vote, and then, in private, they fill in their forms. After the balloting the results are tabulated immediately and announced the same day. If there is no clear winner in the first round, then the two top candidates go in a head-to-head contest. The winner of the most votes makes an acceptance speech and is then given a certificate of power. They have the right to serve for the following three years.

This chapter will look at the history of how this process started, and what the reasons were behind it. It will then look at how elections have been conducted across China, and at the township elections which have risen more recently, and then at what these have achieved, and where they currently stand. As with other areas of reform in China, village elections stand at a crossroads, with new proposals and modifications being made about how they should be developed. But the question of whether they will be taken further into the political system is still stalled.

The village election process: a short history

At the end of the Cultural Revolution much of the infrastructure of governance in China had been decimated. Courts had been destroyed. Many people had simply not been able to attend high school or university, and whole areas of the government and economy did not function. Life in China since the mid-1960s had been intensely politicised, with vicious factional infighting among the elite in Beijing and a series of mass campaigns that had absorbed most people's energy and time.

By Mao's death in early September 1976 the country was exhausted. A mini-uprising only a few months earlier in April the same year, marking grief at Premier Zhou Enlai's death from cancer that January, had been only the most tangible barometer of public weariness at the constant destructive political battles. One of the radical leaders within what was to come to be known as the 'Gang of Four', Zhang Chunqiao, had written a pamphlet as late as 1975 lambasting attempts to reintroduce the poisonous weeds of capitalism into China. In 'On Exercising All Round Dictatorship over the Bourgeoisie' Zhang had declared:

> New bourgeois elements have been engendered batch after batch, and it is precisely the Khrushchev–Brezhnev renegade clique that is their representative. These people generally have a good class background; almost all of them were brought up under the red flag;

they have joined the Communist Party organizationally, received college training and become so-called red experts. However, they are new poisonous weeds engendered by the old soil of capitalism. They have betrayed their own class, usurped Party and state power, restored capitalism, become chieftains of the dictatorship of the bourgeoisie over the proletariat, and accomplished what Hitler had tried to do but failed. Never should we forget this experience of history in which 'the satellites went up to the sky while the red flag fell to the ground', especially not at this time when we are determined to build a powerful country.[1]

Focusing on the issue of collective ownership in the countryside, Zhang had complained that the countryside had become a place where increasingly 'ownership by the whole people ... made up a small proportion'. While collective ownership had increased, the issue of total state domination over industrial and agricultural production still needed to be settled. 'Bourgeois right', Zhang ominously warned, 'has not been totally abolished in this realm'. Now it was time to complete the revolution. 'The extinction of the bourgeoisie and all other exploiting classes and the victory of communism are inevitable, certain and independent of man's will.' Communes and collectivisation in the countryside were to be deepened, not relaxed, and the tiny, shallow roots of private enterprise which Zhang saw emerging in parts of the economy were to be wiped out.

In photographer Liu Heung Shing's excellent collection of images of modern China there is a photo taken by Du Xiuxian in 1976 of a Politburo meeting held a month after the death of Mao in October 1976. It is on the same page as a picture by the same photographer of a sombre-looking Jiang Qing, a fellow member of the Gang of Four, and widow of Mao Zedong. She is in mourning clothes, standing with her back to a garden in what looks to be a shady courtyard.

Both photos are remarkable vignettes of China at a crucial stage of its modern development. Jiang Qing's image, as the photo's caption says, was the last to be taken of her as a free woman. She was arrested the same day, with her fellow Gang members, put on trial in 1981, and sentenced to death, subsequently commuted to life in prison. She was to commit suicide in 1991. The image of the Politburo meeting is even more sobering. In a gloomy room, the meeting table covered over in a white tablecloth, it shows twelve people (eleven men and one woman, Jiang Qing), most of them in Mao suits, their caps placed on the table before them with tea cups and ashtrays sitting among the few papers on the table. Hua Guofeng, for a brief two years the supreme leader of China after Mao, is chairing the meeting. One of the attendees, Zhang Chunqiao, author of the report referred to above, is smoking. The others, the majority of them elderly looking men, are slumped or leaning forward, perfect images of almost detached boredom. Some even look as though they are asleep, though this is hard to confirm, as their backs are towards the camera.[2]

Certainly some of these people firmly supported Zhang's view. The revolution, of which the last ten years had been but a deepening and extension, now needed to be taken even further. Mao's death presented a moment of danger. They had to push even harder for wholesale public ownership of industry and farming. But they were profoundly out of step with the mood of the country. Even as they were meeting, in villages like Fengyang in central Anhui province droughts were causing local leaders to rethink radically the way that they organised agricultural production. The commune system in places like this had led to nothing but grief, failure, famine and death. The old structure of agricultural organisation through production centres, brigades and communes has effectively broken down. There had to be a new way to do things.

With the demise of Mao, the radicals lost their greatest patron. Mao's love of the tactics of divide and rule, creating and then exploiting division in society, had had its day. Only a few weeks after his death, the main leaders, among them the Gang of Four, were taken into custody. Within two years, in late 1978, Deng Xiaoping had stated at the December meeting of the Third Plenary Session of the CCP that,

under our present system of economic management, power is
over-concentrated, so it is necessary to devolve some of it to the
lower levels without hesitation but in a planned way. Otherwise it
will be difficult to give full scope to the initiative of local as well
as national authorities and to the enterprises and workers, and
difficult to practise modern economic management and raise the
productivity of labour.[3]

The most pressing issue was to 'expand the decision-making
powers of mines, factories and other enterprises and of production
teams, so as to give full scope to their initiative and creativity'.
The very individuals and forces in society that were pushing for
private enterprise and for flexibility and pragmatism in economic
policymaking were about to receive a mandate from the highest level.
Zhang had harried the forces of capitalism, calling them 'poison'.
Deng effectively decontaminated them, but his boldest initial moves
were in the rural areas.

If rural China had been the source of Mao's revolution, it had also
borne the brunt of his mad policies. During the Great Leap Forward
in the 1950s 'everything changed. The government kept extracting
food from the countryside, long after it became clear there was no
more to take, while urban dwellers continued to receive at least
some of their grain rations.' The countryside starved in order to
feed the cities. 'An urban household registration had become a meal
ticket, while rural people only had a license to starve.'[4] The need
to do something radical to improve the situation in the countryside
became clearer in the late 1970s, once the radicals had departed the
scene, and indeed most of Deng's early efforts were to address the
huge inequalities that existed in rural China, and to get the economy
there functioning again.

Just like in Fengyang, Anhui, however, other places had already
started to experiment. In Yushan County, Guangxi, a reorganisation
had allowed the establishment of committees to oversee village
administration. In the discussions between 1978 and 1982 before
the publication of a new constitution, there had been debate about

what sort of governance structure might best suit villages. As Shi Tianjian, one of the main scholars of the process of rural democracy has pointed out, decollectivisation, when it came, happened quickly and altered the social structure, redrawing the relationship between the citizens and the state.[5] The constitution, when it was issued, contained in Article 111 the line that 'Village Committees' were to be 'established among urban and rural residents on the basis of their place of residence'. These

> are mass organizations of self-management at the grass-roots level. The chairman, vice-chairmen and members of each residents' or villagers' committee are elected by the residents. The relationship between the residents' and villagers' committees and the grass-roots organs of state power is prescribed by law. The residents' and villagers' committees establish committees for people's media-tion, public security, public health and other matters in order to manage public affairs and social services in their areas, mediate civil disputes, help maintain public order and convey residents' opinions and demands and make suggestions to the people's government.[6]

For such elections there then ensued a five-year discussion period where the precise structure and process were debated. There were three methods contemplated. In the first the Communist Party would maintain control over the Committee by allowing Party bureaucrats from the local branch (the lowest level of Party organisation) to choose the candidates and appoint them. The second would allow county and town government leaders to appoint officials. And the final method, which was the one settled on, would be to hold free and open elections.[7]

As with the establishment of Town and Village Enterprises (TVEs), and the final implementation of the Household Respon-sibility System, allowing farmers to sell surpluses back to the state at a modest profit, there was a significant amount of experimenta-tion in the mid-1980s. In Guangxi, Hubei, and other largely rural provinces there were initial elections. According to one official interviewed in Beijing in August 2009, there had been pilot projects as early as 1980, in over 200 counties. But the results had not been acceptable, and there had been evidence that interest groups had controlled the outcomes of many of these (this will be looked at in more detail in later elections below).[8] Policymakers looked back to 'bean counter' elections in the late 1940s when villagers had simply counted out beans for candidates, with the winner being the one who got most. Another analyst of Chinese elections, however, mentioned the 'Farmers Councils' (*nongmin xiehui*), which had existed into the 1960s before being abandoned, as also being potential models. Elections had even been held in some of the people's communes. Perhaps Lishu in Jilin province can lay claim to be the first time local government had allowed peasant electoral power in the mid-1980s (though some argue that earlier informal elections were held in Guangxi province in 1983).[9]

Whatever the genesis of village elections, as they finally became regulated and institutionalised there was a well-documented and fierce debate in Beijing, with then premier Zhao Ziyang worrying that allowing open elections would create instability in the countryside, and others, particularly Peng Zhen, then head of the NPC, believing that they were a key means to enfranchising a crucial constituency which had been deeply alienated by the experiences of the Cultural Revolution. All this was intensified by the eventual abolishment of communes in 1983, meaning that in effect townships were left running villages, with the local CCP branch expected to govern but with no resources. With Peng Zhen's support the first draft of the Organic Law on Village Elections was prepared in 1986. Defeated the first time at the NPC, it was finally passed in 1987, and, ironically, in view of the defeat of the Tiananmen Square protests in 1989, implemented from that year. As one analyst said, 'From 1988, village elections have become a process of systematic democratisation.'[10]

What does the law say?

While the 1982 Constitution, Article 111, gives ultimate sanction to self-administration for villages, the formal legal basis for village elections is in two laws: 'The Organic Law of the Villagers Committee of the People's Republic of China (for Trial Implementation)', adopted by the NPC in 1987, and the full 'Organic Law of the Villagers Committee of the PRC', passed over ten years later in 1998. The initial law stated in its preamble that it had been brought in

> with a view to ensuring self-government by the villagers in the countryside, who will administer their own affairs in accordance with the law, and promoting socialist democracy at the grassroots level, socialist material development, and the building of an advanced socialist culture and ideology in the rural areas.[11]

It says that the Village Committee will be an organisation of self-government, regulating the affairs of those within the community, working under the government of the nearest township. Article 5 of the original law asks that Village Committees observe the law, and promote lawfulness among those living in the village. Article 7 sets out the numbers of those who can serve on a committee (from three to seven), reporting to the Village Assembly, and accountable to them. It also stipulates that committees 'give full play to democracy, carefully heed dissenting opinions and shall not resort to coercion and commandism or retaliation'. This was a prudent nod to the possibility that those who were successful in gaining power might be tempted to use their new position to settle grievances from the recent and often bitter past.

Modern peasant uprisings: Renshou County, Sichuan

Rural discontent has not magically disappeared as a result of the liberalisation of China's economy in the last decades. Inequality has soared and there remain stark differences between the developed western areas and impoverished inland ones. Economist Yasheng

Huang argues that China enjoyed a decade of great liberalism in the 1980s, what he calls an 'explosion of indigenous, completely private entrepreneurship', where banks were able to lend reasonably freely, and officials, on the whole, gave the non-state sector a lot of space. According to Huang, the most striking feature of this was that 'almost all this entrepreneurship occurred in the rural areas of the country'.[12] The violent shock of 1989 scared the central government into placing far more restrictions on the non-state sector, especially in rural areas, tightening up lending criteria and increasing the role of the state. When entrepreneurism restarted in the 1990s it was in a subtly different guise, with the state operating a 'political pecking order', favouring state entities over private ones through regulations, banking support and official sanction.

China may have grown richer over the ensuing years but in many cases its farmers did not see massive benefits. A famous report by two Anhui journalists in 2001 (quickly banned in China itself) discussed one particular area of grievances – taxes. 'According to the statistics of the government's Department for Supervising the Peasants' Burdens, there are ninety-three categories of fees and charges, funds and reserves, devised by the State Council.'[13] Needless to say, this was a source of great discontent for many in rural areas and something that the central government sought to address by abolishing most of these payments in the late 2000s. Levies unilaterally placed on farmers were behind one of the most celebrated examples of mass unrest in recent years, the Renshou County riots in Sichuan Province, which took place between mid-May and early June 1993. Initially around a thousand peasants took to the streets protesting at demands by the local government for an ad hoc tax to build a highway in their district. Wielding rods and scythes, and throwing rocks, they attacked local officials, whose first attempts to deal with the problem only resulted in some 10,000 (half the population of the county) coming out to protest. Things were eventually resolved when a deputy governor of the province ordered the tax to be lifted and what money had already been paid to be returned to the farmers.[14]

Such anti-tax riots were all too common in the years leading up to the formal issuing of the full Organic Law in 1998. Cheng and Wu in their report cover in detail one such in 1997 in Gao village, Lingbi

County in Anhui, prompted by local anger at the heavy-handed antics of the village strongman, also called Gao. Massive disturbances in the village were dealt with by violence, police intervention, and the detention of most of those believed to be the ringleaders. The local Party chief specifically openly tortured and beat up a son of one of the protestors, effectively silencing anyone else who might have fancied their chances of causing trouble. As Chen and Wu caustically comment, 'The Gao Village incident had taken place in broad daylight and had been witnessed by hundreds of people. How can people's mouths be sealed by threats and arrests... Can you lie to all the people all of the time?'[15] In some parts of contemporary China, it seemed that you could.

The 1998 law is formulated in a slightly different way to the provisional earlier one. It speaks of 'developing democracy at the grassroots level in the countryside, and promoting the building of a socialist countryside which is materially and ethically advanced'.[16] It spells out the role for the CCP, a vexed question which we will come back to later, by stating that

the primary organization of the Communist Party of China in the countryside shall carry out its work in accordance with the Constitution of the Communist Party of China, playing its role as a leading nucleus; and, in accordance with the Constitution and laws, support the villagers and ensure that they carry out self-government activities and exercise their democratic rights directly.

The Village Committees 'assist the government in their work', administering 'affairs concerning the land and other property collectively owned'. Like the 1987 law, the 1998 law sets out the number of people who can sit on a committee, their responsibilities to the Village Assembly, and stresses the need for fair representation of women and ethnic minorities. It also clarifies the procedural rules for elections (secret ballot, with more candidates than positions to be filled) and also the process whereby an office holder can be removed.

The 1998 law is, unsurprisingly, far more detailed in spelling out the responsibilities of Village Committees. It allows office holders to be part of the production process (i.e. work), even though, once elected, at least the Village Committee head gets a wage (one of the main attractions in some areas for standing for the position.) It also stipulates that not just some but all villages should hold elections. In that sense it sets out a universal vision for grassroots democracy in the country.

Why village elections?

There is one more historic question to answer. In view of the fact that China, at least in rural areas, had a relatively shallow experience of universal-franchise elections and democratic experimentation, why were rural areas alone chosen to introduce this new method? It seems contradictory to promote a fairly advanced system in some of the most deprived, backward areas of China, often among people with very low levels of education, many of whom were illiterate. Linda Jacobson argues that in fact the leaders who decided this at a central level in the 1980s had many reasons to do what they did. Beyond the breakdown of governance in the villages in the 1960s and 1970s, there was also the issue of Village Committees having to do what she calls 'the state's dirty work'. They had to implement very unpopular local and national family-planning restrictions (these became much tighter in the 1980s) and then deal with tax collecting and the laying off of some workers from the state agricultural system. These were functions that only those with some kind of clear mandate could easily carry out. Elections were seen as a straightforward way of at least making sure that they did have this legitimacy among those they were about to deal with.

There was another, more Party-orientated, reason. The CCP needed some mechanism by which to talent-spot people who were likely to be good potential Party members. The Party's ranks were depleted after a decade of self-destruction from the mid-1960s onwards. It needed new administrators from the grassroots. According to one estimate, of the non-Party members who stood in the elections 80 per cent were then recruited to join the Party.[17] This fits in with the 'co-option or repression' strategy that the Party has adopted in the last decades. Village elections were a good way to get new blood into the CCP.

There were other reasons for elections. One was to do something about the endemic corruption among local elites in rural China – people who were starting to rise up through doing business, or who had strong family links or networks in specific areas. Elections were seen as introducing notions of accountability, so that those who failed to perform were somehow prised out of their local fiefdoms. The appearance of local strongmen who were able to dominate in some regions by building up supporters around them has been one of the cancers of modern Chinese politics. In the 1920s and 1930s, before war brutally enforced some semblance of unity, China was afflicted by almost chronic regionalism. Warlords ran whole stretches of the country, accountable only to themselves and the other elites around them. The CCP sincerely intended as part of the thinking behind elections to grant those who were least powerful in the country some control over their leaders. The results, however, have been variable, and the battle for transparent, accountable government, even at this level, continues, as will be shown later.

There is one final reason, which was perhaps wholly unintended. The village election process has in effect been a massive act of education that has taught over 800 million people, over two decades, the principles of Party and non-Party members running for power, of secret ballots, and of one person, one vote. It has also taught the principles of universal suffrage and of a choice of candidates. Village elections were not meant to be the seeds of anything else. But perhaps one day their introduction may be seen as a hugely significant moment when ideas of government being accountable to people who had the power to vote them in or out of power started to take root.

Down to the countryside: Yali village

Yali village is only two hours by bus and then taxi from the outskirts of Beijing. And yet even at the end of the first decade of the twenty-first century it might as well be on another planet. The village has a population of just under 300, living in traditional houses, next to agricultural land. As we park the car, a group of elder residents, sitting by a tree in the small square at the centre of the cluster of old, dusty buildings, fall silent when they see a foreigner step out. A dog lies next to a muddy wall. The wall has a slogan in large white characters written across it, extolling the importance of family planning. 'I came to this place in the Cultural Revolution', Ms Wang, the woman with me, says. She is in her late forties. 'I haven't been back since. It hasn't changed a lot.' A man with a disability goes by. 'They had that problem back then', she says, looking at him. 'Too much inbreeding. Very high incidence of deformities.'

She leads us to the house she thinks she stayed in then, through a round, traditional-style gate, into a garden growing corn cobs. Another black dog lies on the path to the open door of the single-storey house ahead. We go in without knocking, and see an old man, sitting on the *kang*, the brick-built platform in the living room that doubles, at night, as a bedroom. The decor is flaking and dirty but there is a huge, new television, in pride of place, against the west wall of the house.

The old man is in his late seventies. His accent is very thick, hard to understand at first. Ms Wang tells him that we have come to learn more about village elections and how they have gone on here. The old man snorts. He was the Village Committee head in the 1990s. He had been elected twice. Then he nods at a large, newer white building just over the wall from his own. 'That's the offices for the new guy. He's no good. Just lined his own pockets. Came back from being a businessman elsewhere, but now he's making a packet here. Hardly ever see him.'

Can unproposed candidates stand in elections? I ask. 'What's the point?', he says. 'They never get elected if the town government and the Party don't support them. You're just storing up grief if you put one of those in power.'

The township is important. This village, like almost every other in China, gets almost all its financial subventions from it. 'We have 150 thousand yuan (US$21,963) a year from them', the old man says. 'The village head gets 1,200 yuan (US$175.7) a month. But they get a stack more for official entertainment.' He snorts again. 'They might as well consider that a gift. There is no accountability about how they spend it.'

What about the relationship between the Party boss of the village and the village head? 'They come along and explain Party policy, but in this place they are in the pocket of the head. It's different in other villages around here. In some the Party head is number one, in others it's the village head. Depends on the person and the place.'

From time to time new graduates are sent down to help administer the village. 'It is meant to give them experience', he says. But none of them stays long. Like their predecessors, the seconded youths of the Cultural Revolution years who were despatched to isolated undeveloped places to learn about real life outside the cities, they spend most of their time working out how to get back to where they came from.

'Does the village election give you a real choice?' I ask. He looks at me hard, realising perhaps for the first time I am not just an outsider, even though non-Chinese. 'There are no real choices in elections', he scoffs. 'None at all.'

We go to the offices next door. There are a group of people round a small table, playing mah-jong, slightly startled by our arrival. 'These must be the other committee members', Ms Wang says. She asks one of them, an elderly man, where the village head is. 'Out on business', he says. But he grabs a primitive mobile phone and calls, barking down some words about 'people here to see you'. The man at the other end of the call is in fact only a few minutes away, in a large, new hotel built on the edge of the district. 'You'll find him there', he says, watching us go.

We drive to a stark white new building with ceramic tiles and large tinted windows. It is a hotel and restaurant combined. Mr Li is on the first floor, in one of the VIP rooms, having lunch with seven other men. As we go up the stairs we can hear their laughter. 'This place is brand new', Ms Wang says, looking around her. 'It has definitely been built after the rules came in about no longer using agricultural land for non-farming enterprises.' She tuts. 'Why on earth would they need a big place like this in a tiny village at the back of beyond?'

Mr Li is red-faced through drinking the strong local white spirit. Everyone else has been drinking it too, and the room smells strongly of its fumes as we walk in. But he is hospitable and asks us, the moment we appear, to sit down. 'We want to understand village elections', Ms Wang says, somewhat directly. But he is unfazed. 'Sure, what do you want to know?'

I start off by asking him about his background. He was local, he says, but went off in the 1990s to make money elsewhere. He is a businessman. 'It is good that practical people like us are allowed to stand. We can sort problems out more easily. We have a wider experience of life.'

And the relationship between the Party secretary and the village head? Having them as one, like they do in some places, 'at least avoids conflict', Li says. 'After all, the head of the Village Committee is the legal person. They are responsible in law. If anyone sues, then it is the name of the village head not the Party boss that appears on the court documents. We are the ones who have to appear in court. But on many issues the Party boss takes the final decision. We're held accountable for their decisions. It is risky. They have power and no responsibility.'

He is distracted by his friends, who are ready for another drink. 'I've been in this job since 2006', he says.

Who is the Party boss of this village? I ask before we go.

He laughs. 'Me of course. I wouldn't have dared be village head without being Party head too. Wasn't that clear in what I said just now?'[18]

Elections on the edges: Yunnan

If elections were to restore some level of accountability and stability to the governance of remote parts of China, then a key area they needed to deliver in were some of the most isolated border regions inhabited by China's ethnic minorities. When the PRC was established in 1949 it inherited a particular view of Han and non-Han inhabitants of the country, much of it which arose from a complex history of territorial expansion reaching back over a thousand years. Founder of the Nationalist Party and, briefly, its first president, Dr Sun Yat-sen had mentioned five ethnic groups in his work: Han, Muslim, Tibetan, Mongolian and Uyghur. But the Communists aimed for a more expanded sense of ethnicity, increasing the number of recognised minorities to fifty-five. The ways in which they did this were somewhat arbitrary, with there being good arguments that some of the defined groups in Yunnan, the huge province in the south-west of the country, could be broken down even further.

All of China's fifty-five ethnic minorities are guaranteed equality before the law, and indeed the constitution of the PRC states that China is a 'multi-ethnic state'. Nevertheless, there is an overwhelming dominance of Han Chinese – officially 93 per cent of the whole population. There are valid questions to be asked about just how cohesive this massive group is. But whatever differences might exist between different types of Han Chinese, these are relatively slight compared to the huge distinctions between some of the other fifty-five and the Han majority. Language, appearance, religion, social habits all differ from the Han in some cases. In Yunnan, for example, there is a richly diverse culture in an area that has only with difficulty been brought into the great zone of influence and then sovereignty of what is now the centralised PRC state. In living memory it has experienced conflicts and impulses to pull away from the Beijing government. Development and settlement from other areas of China, as with other ethnic-minority regions, has only brought an uneasy allegiance. In much of rural Yunnan, ethnic minorities dominate.

According to researcher Goran Leijonhufvud, who spent time from 2004 to 2006 looking at the process of village elections in areas of Yunnan in south-west China dominated by ethnic minorities, particularly the Yi ethnic group, elections suffered from particular challenges both in how they were implemented and in how their

outcomes were seen in these areas.[19] Lack of development, high levels
of illiteracy and a range of other factors meant that elections faced
particular challenges, in terms of how they were administered and
what they meant for those in the areas they were held in. Scepticism
about the possibility of running any kind of plebiscite in areas
where many lack even basic education is high among, in particular,
urban elites. But Leijonhufvud's observations showed that there
were very specific issues raised by these elections, only partly due
to the suspicion that these were connected to some grand project of
sinification promoted by agents of the central state.

Like the national story, there was a memory of elections being
held in the 1920s, when Yi nationality members practised voting for
the headmen (*hou tou*) and the village elder, the first responsible for
administration and the second for social order. In the years before
the 1949 revolution villages were broken down into neighbourhoods
of twenty-five households, and then household groups often, but
this granular structure was all but destroyed in the 1950s as land
reformation and reallocation occurred. In two villages, one of over
2,500 people, and the other of 800, Leijonhufvud was able to look
at the conduct of village elections in the new structure brought in
after 1981 when the village communes had been dismantled. In an
economy dominated by tobacco production, the chief issue in all of
the elections was the taxes that were likely to be levied on crops, the
need to build roads that could transport the goods out of the area,
and some issues around mining and tourism. At heart, therefore,
economic considerations were uppermost in people's minds as they
looked at who to vote for.

As in elections in the central Shanxi province area, however, the
implementation and process caused the main problems. At the election
Leijonhufvud was present at, no one was allowed to make speeches;
this, the township authorities in charge of the election stated, was
'to stop them making unrealistic promises'. The dense network of
relationships in the village community meant that people voted more
for the person standing and who they were linked to than or any

specific issues, no matter how important these were. As one official remarked, 'The common people do not care about the qualities or characters of the candidates. All they care about is relations.'

Beyond this social issue was a more administrative one. At least in terms of what might be loosely called constituencies, villages were not natural communities but, rather, large areas which consisted of a number of settled areas, many of them large in their own right. This created a number of headaches. Small hamlets or settlements were marginalised by larger ones, which managed to return chosen candidates because of a natural bloc-voting bias. More problematic even than this was the common phenomenon of proxy voting, something that also happened in Han-dominated areas. In a society which was once, for the brief years under Mao, highly static, with the only movement allowed that sanctioned by the central state in its immense relocation programmes, and where every citizen was given an internal passport (the *Hukou* – household registration document), in the reform period China has become a country of immense social movement. It is estimated that there are 200 million migrant workers (the *mang liu* – blind flow) who have moved to cities and urbanising areas to work in factories, construction sites or in the entertainment sector (for an estimated 7 million women that means prostitution). This vast army comes from the rural areas, like these villages in Yunnan. In their absence (and a large number simply never return), fellow villagers are allowed to vote on their behalf. This is set at a limit of three proxy votes per person. Leijonhufvud, in a simple survey, was able to show that of a sample of 119 votes cast, 48 were done directly and 68 by proxy. In one case, someone was voting for 20 other people.

Nor was it just for absent voters that people stood in. There was a high incidence of men voting for all the other members of their households, of parents voting for their grown-up children, and of relatives voting for their families who were either out working in the fields, or who simply could not be bothered to turn up. Often the head of a household voted for everyone under one roof. Women

voted far less than men, which compounded the problems recognised by the central government of a lack of female representation
on Village Committees and as village leaders. The Communist Party
nationally, however, is on shaky ground here, as only 19 per cent of
its own members are female, and only one woman currently sits in
the full Politburo, among twenty-four men.

This small survey in an ethnic-minority area shows quite easily
some of the major problems of trying to run elections in areas which
have the social, economic and cultural issues that Yunnan villages
have. According to an administrator on the 2000–2006 EU China
village governance scheme, one of the largest foreign assistance
projects, the issues were largely ones which were dealt with by
education. On this scheme, a number of Village Committee heads
from ethnic-minority areas were enrolled on courses in Beijing. For
many of them it was their first visit to the capital, let alone being
exposed to European experts talking about how best to make their
administrations efficient and to run elections smoothly. It was not
clear which part of this visit was the more traumatic!

Lurking behind the generic issues that elections in ethnic-minority
areas bring up is the sense of deep residual suspicion on the part
of the upper levels of government, both in the province and in the
capital, that these might offer a vehicle for expression of separatist
intent. Villages dominated by specific minorities, either in Xinjiang
Autonomous Region, where there is a large proportion of Uyghur
Muslims, or in Inner Mongolia, where the 10 per cent of the local
population that are Mongolian are disproportionally based in isolated areas on the grasslands, might well see elections as a means
whereby discontent about ethnic issues comes through in results.
With its stress on harmony and unity, this is something the central
government is deeply anxious about, and any attempt therefore to
hijack such elections for what might look like any purpose antithetic
to the CCP at the centre would be stubbed out swiftly.

It is not just allegiances based on ethnic identity that cause
problems. Tribalism occurs in the form of family allegiance in some

areas, with those with the surname Wang all voting in one bloc, and those with the surname Li in another. Breaking these links in a society which is famed for its densely embedded and established networks is next to impossible. On top of this there is the issue of the very culture of voting, with people keen to demonstrate solidarity, and so choosing to hold votes in public rather than in private booths. This runs to the heart of the often stated desire in Chinese public life to aim for consensus before implementing a solution, rather than imposing one before this consensus has been reached, which might cause disharmony and conflict.

Enfranchisement in the cities: residence committees

China is one of the few societies that has experienced reverse urbanisation. In the great Maoist campaigns from the 1950s to the 1970s, large swathes of people were relocated from the cities to parts of the countryside that were deemed to need redevelopment. There was approximately a 2 per cent fall in the population of cities over this period. But by 1980 the trend was reversing. Many of those who had been sent down were able to return to their original place of residence. By the late 1980s China was in the throes of a vast process of urbanisation. This has only intensified in the last two decades. While the official statistics state that a small majority of Chinese still live in the countryside, anyone travelling around China will notice that large parts of the country look pretty urban, even while they are described as villages or rural settlements. As in Japan, most of the vast eastern coast is intensively occupied and built up. Cities like Beijing and Shanghai have rocketed from populations of around 7 or 8 million apiece in the last years of Mao to vast conurbations with, in Shanghai's case, over 19 million people. These cities reach out from their original territory, encroaching on towns and cities nearby to create megacities. There is already talk of Hangzhou, Nanjing and Shanghai creating one such epic city, stretching across three provinces and linked by a high speed train, which is due to open in 2011, collapsing the travelling distance between these points from hours down to a matter of minutes.

Such a highly fluid, mobile society has meant that cities also have a huge number of newcomers, people who are moving in to work not only in manual trades, but also professionally. Many more Chinese now go to university. Once only 1 per cent were graduates, as was the case as recently as 1994; now the figure is creeping closer to 6 or 7 per cent. Graduate unemployment became a potential headache for the government after the global economic downturn in 2008. The old system of work units allocating jobs for everyone is long gone. Today there is an open market, much like in the West, where people have to apply for work, and in some sectors face stiff competition.

Those who manage to find work can then buy property. Shanghai and Beijing, along with every other fair-sized city or town in China, has seen the construction of many billions of square feet of residential property. House ownership has been one of the great generators of wealth for Chinese entrepreneurs, just as it has in the West, with the *Fortune* rich lists produced over the last decade each year dominated by people who have made their riches through property development. The Cambridge-educated Zhang Xin, with her husband Pan Shiyi, is one of the most successful of China's new breed of property developers, running Soho, a company that has rebuilt large sections of Beijing, and that is now reaching out into the rest of the country. There are many others.

The new professionals come to communities in cities and towns where there is no sense of history, and almost nothing of community. This has been a problem. Urban ghettos are starting to appear with worrying frequency, bringing with them all the problems that happened in the West. Levels of depression and violence have risen, running against the grain of a society which is highly networked, and where personal contact is prized. Marx spoke about alienation, but he meant of man from the fruits of his labour. In contemporary China, the Marxist ideological landscape has changed, but there is a new form of alienation, where people from vastly different communities resettle in areas with which they have no bonds or connection except through their work.

The flip side of elections in villages, therefore, has been similar one-person, one-vote residential committee elections for districts, or even accommodation blocks in cities. Wandering into one large block in the summer of 2010 in central Beijing I noticed photos of the residence committee members placed on a notice board with their names and responsibilities. In theory, these committees, which have been run in Shanghai at least since 1999, and are being rolled out across the rest of the country, should create cohesion and a sense of society. They deal with rubbish collection, security, the upkeep of public spaces around the residential area, provision of childcare, and so on. Many of these issues, in fact, were handled by the old Neighbourhood Committees which existed under Mao, although there they famously had a much more intrusive role, dictating how people lived their lives, spying, and sometimes applying tremendous social pressure on residents. In the Cultural Revolution, these committees in cities that were dominated by radicals, like Shanghai, were turned over to activists, who used them to invade the most intimate spaces of people's lives, ransacking houses, assembling those accused of thought crimes for struggle sessions, during which those accused of political crimes were placed before an audience and abused, humiliated, and even killed. These Neighbourhood Watch Committees were one of the key means by which people's private lives were then interfered with and intruded upon.

That may well be why such committees languished for many years. In the 1980s urban residents wanted politics out of their lives as much as possible. Weary of the constant campaigns of prior decades they got on with making money and enjoying the new economic liberties granted them. Now things have moved on. Residents in suburban China want a better quality of life. They want to feel enfranchised, at least as far as their living environment goes. Municipal authorities have granted districts in Shanghai the right to hold residence committee elections. According to Liu Chunrong, an academic at Fudan University in Shanghai who has studied these committees, they have 'revitalised' decision-making in the areas where they are held. Motivated by the fear of too great a level of alienation, the government has used these committees, much like those in the countryside, to assert levels of control.

One retired government official in Beijing who talked to me about the elections for residence committees in their area in August 2009 complained, however, that they were 'purely for the unemployed, the retired and the mentally ill'. He said that such committees had no power or function and no budget over which to exercise control. The little money they do control is the small management fee levied by some of the districts. Even this, complained the official, offered scope for corruption. 'In China', he stated, 'democracy is better in the villages than in the cities.' Residence committee elections 'have no connection with daily life'.

It is somewhat paradoxical that elections are seen as being more vibrant in the countryside, in view of the snobbery of city people towards the rural population (not that China is alone in this phenomenon – most countries have their versions of *tu baozi*, 'potato dumplings' – or country bumpkins). Sinologist Linda Jakobson records the disdainful statement of one official on the holding of elections in villages. 'Teaching democracy to peasants is like playing the piano to cows.'[20] Perhaps it is a sign of the Party not taking governance at village level seriously that it has allowed experimentation. Or it might be that it is precisely because the Party fears disturbances at the village level that it has allowed enfranchisement this way, confident of its ability to control the risks better this way.

Township elections

The great aspiration has always been that one day village elections would be extended to townships. Townships, after all, are a formal part of government structures. Having elections at this level would be highly meaningful. Semi-competitive township elections were first

The township congress activist

While Village Committees and residence committees form one part of the structure of governance in the PRC, there is another – that of the congresses, which extend from township, up to county, prefecture, province and then national levels. Direct elections are held for congress members only at the two lowest levels – those of town and county. For all the others, indirect elections are held. The first law mandating this was passed as early as 1954, though since then there have been a number of modifications, the most recent of which was at the National People's Congress in 2010, allowing equal representation at congresses of rural and urban residents. Before this there had been a bias against rural-area representatives.

The constituencies for congress members are highly variable. A constituency might be a factory, a district in a city, or an area of land. In the 1980s independents started to attempt to stand for election to congresses. While membership grants no major powers, a congress at least has some law-making influence, and is a legitimate basis for protests about local and national issues (the NPC was, for instance, one of the main places where opposition to the Three Gorges Dam was most vocal in the 1990s). And congress members at all levels do get the right to voice objections to official reports.

As in village elections, the town and county congress elections are meant to be one person, one vote, and are open to non-Party members. Nevertheless, it took until 1998 for the first true independent, a social activist called Yao Lifa, to get onto a township congress in Qianjiang City, Hubei. He was voted off after claims of intimidation and vote-rigging in 2003, and failed in his last attempt for re-election, in 2006. But by this time his example had encouraged others to join in, with Lu Banglie, also in Hubei, being the most prominent. 'While in office', as American academic Joseph Fewsmith noted, 'Yao was an energetic thorn in the side of the local government. He alone raised 187 of the 459 suggestions, opinions and criticisms presented to the local people's congress over the five year term.' Less positively, Yao also undertook a survey of the 329 villages within Qianjiang area, and found that 269 of these had seen committee members elected in 1999 subsequently dismissed for malpractice.[21]

held in 1995. Almost at the same time as the Organic Law for Village Elections was passed in 1998, the first township chief was elected, in Baoshi Town, Suining City, Sichuan. Sichuan was to prove to be an incubator for other successful ballots, with follow-ups occurring in December 1998 and early 1999. By 2002, over 200 Township Committees had people on them who had been through some kind of electoral process. Fujian, Henan, Shanxi and Guangdong also experienced these. As Hong Kong-based academic Simon Shen observed, 'Not only would town-level direct elections mark the next stage of reform in self-governance in the Chinese countryside, but also represent a great leap in China's democratisation.'[22] In 1999, Dapeng, a township in the newly built city of Shenzhen, Guangdong province, had an elected committee. But the process was stopped in 2002.

Since then, there have been only very partial and ad hoc subsequent elections, using a number of different models. According to the *China Daily*, Lingshan township, also in Sichuan, was the first to pilot direct elections for the CCP local committee in 2001, an experiment which was then tentatively extended to Caiqi town in Jiangsu in 2003. According to an academic at the Central Party School, Lu Xianfu, these precedents 'smashed the long established practice of CCP officials being nominated by superior party organisations.'[23] Lai Hairong, an official based in Beijing, explained that the positions open to partially competitive elections included that of township governor, and his or her deputy. These had usually been purely appointed by the County Party Committee, the next level of administration up. However, in some areas in China, in the early 2000s, a partial system was allowed, whereby those who were nominated to the Country Committee and then approved were sent to the townships to gain approval via an electoral process involving the community there. As with village elections, the process was highly controlled. In township elections candidates had to be Party members. They were allowed to make speeches at the final hustings before the election itself, and in theory they were allowed to nominate themselves, but this proved to be rare in practice.

In the end it was largely dependent on the local county whether township elections happened and how far they went. By 2004, they had become increasingly rare.[24]

Shen identifies a number of problems in the direct election of township executives. Conflicts between towns and the counties in charge of them are common, with the same tensions between Party functionaries and elected ones – what has been called 'intra-governmental alienation'. Directly elected township executives also have experienced conflict with the elected Village Committee heads over whom they have control. Finally there are tensions with the local congresses.[25] There is a general lack of clarity over what powers elected executives have, and no nationally accepted rules. From 2004 it has generally been accepted that the centre had concentrated on creating intra-Party democracy (see below). Perhaps surprisingly, in May 2010 Shenzhen announced once more that it was going to introduce elections for Party positions, something that had been tentatively suggested some years before but quietly put on the back burner. A report from the official government news service Xinhua stated that rather than upper levels of the Party picking city committees, there would be competitive elections. If this indeed happens, then Shenzhen will prove to be as innovative in governance as it has been economically.[26]

Foreign support and monitoring of elections

Discussing village elections in the summer of 2009 with a range of people – NGO workers, academics, officials – I was struck by the general agreement that foreign support had been important in setting up the whole process of elections and in improving them. The European Union, the Ford Foundation and the Carter Center, along with other outside organisations, had all been involved in monitoring and assessing elections. As one technical assistance expert said,

> People don't understand how complicated holding even a simple election is. What sort of ballot sheets do you have, how do you arrange people's names, where are the ballots put, what sort of

secret booth can you have, especially in very poor areas where there are very limited resources? When do you count the votes, and how do you announce them? How do you deal with disputes, and who is responsible if there are claims of malpractice? This is just on the day of the election. The run-up is even more complex. Elections are a difficult business.

Programmes were run to help officials deal with voting. Some of the earliest, in the 1990s, were instrumental in creating the whole process. But when asked whether this sort of assistance could be maintained, there was a sense that what had been doable was already achieved. As another observer said, 'Until the Chinese central government takes the decision to scale elections up to higher levels of government, then there is little more we can do.'

The Carter Center in particular offers an excellent case study of how foreign assistance in the conduct of elections has fared. Its report from one of the earlier elections in 1997 begins with the simple statement:

> Despite problems, the village elections are important, first, because the election law mandates the basic norms of a democratic process – secret ballot, direct election, multiple candidates, public count, 3-year fixed term – and the Ministry of Civil Affairs is trying hard to implement these norms throughout the country. Second, as each village repeats the process, China widens and deepens its technical capacity to hold elections. Third, the government is open to exchanging views as to the best way to implement the election rules, and the delegation offered 14 specific suggestions on ways to improve the process, including by standardizing the rules and employing a county- or province-wide civic education program.[27]

Where the buck stops: the Party versus elected heads

Mao Zedong's great love of contradiction is enshrined in one of his few purely abstract philosophical works. 'On Contradiction' was quoted exhaustively during the political campaigns of the 1950s and 1960s. It served as the perfect accompaniment to the grinding, divisive class-struggle movements which reached their apogee in the Cultural Revolution. 'The law of contradictions in things', Mao opined in 1937, 'that is, the law of the unity of opposites, is the basic law of nature, and society, and also the basic law of thought.'[28] It is not surprising therefore that, to this day, Chinese society and political structures remain profoundly contradictory, in view of the fact that they were founded on a social philosophy which partly celebrated this. Perhaps the greatest of all these contradictions is that between the role of the Party and other social institutions, including those for governance. There is still no clear constitutional divide between where the functions of the Party end and those of the structures in particular of governance start, despite promises early on to do so. This lies at the heart of the unease expressed by the delegates from the Carter Center in 1996 over the relationship between Party branch heads and Village Committee leaders. Every village they would have gone to would have had a Party branch. There would have been a Party secretary, sometimes the same person standing for election to the Village Committee. How, in the end, could the responsibilities between the elected village heads and the Party head be harmonised?

Most analysts, Chinese or otherwise, admit that there is no straightforward answer to this. The issues it raises go to the heart of the vision of political reform growing out of elections, as discussed in Chapter 5. In the last few years there have been a number of attempts, at local and national levels, to resolve this tension. But, as one academic in Beijing noted in 2009,

> In some places the two work together and there is no problem. In others it is all out war. In still others, the Village Committee head is the real boss, because of his social prestige, whether he is a Party member or not. It all depends on the context. There are no hard and fast rules.

In theory, the Party branch secretary is in charge of the Party line. He (or occasionally she) will be there with their deputy to ensure that Party policy is not contradicted, and that ideological work is undertaken. They look after the Party members and ensure that Party work carries on. One of the great achievements of the CCP is to have penetrated to this level in Chinese society. Unlike any other organisation, they have a presence at the most elementary social levels. This has been the case since the 1950s when the CCP rose to power on its ability to organise and embed itself in the countryside. A leading intellectual in Beijing pointed out in May 2010 that the CCP was, in fact, different from the Communist Party in the Soviet Union, which had simply not existed in this way. Factories and villages might have had Party members, and Party organisations, but nothing as universal as the structures which are now in place in the PRC for the Party. It is, as a famous traditional Chinese song says, like the air one breathes or the water in which fish swim, ubiquitously present.

The increasing complexity of Chinese society, its modernisation, and the need for forms of accountability and responsibility have not been avoidable. In the last thirty years, therefore, the PRC has seen a wave of reforms intended to change the structure of government and make it clearer who does what. Central government ministries have been reduced from almost fifty departments down to thirty. Vested interests have been attacked. This is an ongoing process, but it is motivated by the need for administrative reform, something fit for purpose for a modernising society and a modern economy. Village elections have not been immune from this. The powers that Village Committees have over at least the disbursement of land rights, if nothing else, means that they have to operate with a level of public support. But there are plenty of cases of Party branch secretaries viewing these elections as a threat, trying to stop people standing who might compete with them, or simply obstructing the whole process. It is at times like this that the CCP seems a lobby group for its own interests and can put up a formidable struggle.

This has been dealt with in a number of ways. In some areas the *yi ba shou* ('Party secretary as number one') has been adopted, creating an immediate power hierarchy. Shandong province has seen the *yijian tiao* ('carrying on one shoulder') method, whereby the Party in the township nominates the Party branch secretary as the Village Commitee candidate, who then combines the two positions. This is a development of the 'two ballots rule' (*liang piao zhi*), whereby both Party and non-Party members vote in the first raft of elections, and then only Party members vote on those who received support from more than 50 per cent of voters in the first round. 'Carrying on one shoulder', however, creates an obvious problem. Despite having the support of the central government, these methods 'may harm village self governance in the long run.... Higher level organisations have the incentive to intervene, and manipulate the election' in order to see their chosen candidates returned.[29]

Conclusion

Despite the enormous amount of data on elections, there is still a great deal about their process, function and the role they play in society that needs to be clearer before we can be certain about how successful they have been at addressing the issues of stability and development in the countryside. Most observers accept that in half the places in which they have been held, they have been successful. But in other areas they have been a cause of further discontent. As Joseph Fewsmith has stated, 'These elections have created tensions between Party and Village Committees.' In some areas they have become a site of contention between different groups. They reflect the society in ferment around them. Elections at this level have an eerie ambiguity. Are they a sop by the Party to give the outward appearance of reform, while inwardly only bolstering its powers? For minority areas, are they really delivering self-governance, or are they a way to aid encroaching sinification? Have they been a means of empowerment or a way for the Party to spot talented administrators and then recruit them? Has the foreign assistance given to conduct and then develop such elections led merely to a dead end, or has it provided the groundwork for deeper engagement between China and the outside world? The final question is the toughest one to answer. Are these elections really democratic or merely a charade? And even if the former is the case, can the Party ultimately control the forces that its experiment might unleash? It is now time to turn to what Chinese themselves are saying about these issues, in the great debate about reform in the modern PRC.

China's Mr Democracy: Li Fan

On the edges of the fourth ring road of Beijing near the Asian Games Village built to host this event in 1990, only a year after China was emerging from international isolation after the Tiananmen Square uprising in 1989, is the office of the World China Institute. Founded in 1993, according to its own introductory brochure by 'a group of scholars, civil servants, policy analysts and intellectuals', its goal has been 'to fully develop into a first-class think-tank on public policy'. But the heart and soul of the Institute is Mr Li Fan, who modestly describes himself as 'a productive writer and a brilliant thinker'.

Finding Mr Li's office is not easy. The taxi drops one by a post office on a busy interchange running north. From there, one can walk into a large estate with dozens of white residential skyscrapers. While Mr Li reassures one on the phone that the office is 'dead easy to find', in fact only after a large detour is it possible to track down the entrance to his block and get in the lift to the 14th floor.

Li was profiled by *Time* magazine in 2004. Born the year of the revolution, in 1949, he has good links to the elite in the founding generation of Party members. His father was close to former Premier Zhou Enlai. He attended an elite school. During the Cultural Revolution, almost as a rite of passage, he was a revolutionary Red Guard agitating in Beijing. His partner then was modern China's most prominent dissident, Wei Jingsheng. But while the Beijing Zoo electrician was to step over the line and offend paramount leader Deng Xiaoping during the Democracy Wall movement in 1978, Li stayed out of trouble, going off to the United States to study for five years before he was recalled to China, according to *Time* by then Party secretary Zhao Ziyang in 1989, just months before the Tiananmen Square uprising. Li kept his distance from the democracy movement of 1989, saying that the tragic outcome, with students shot in the Square and a huge clampdown afterwards, 'confirmed for me that radical action would never succeed'.

Since 1993, Li has built his small NGO into one of the most productive and active on governance in China. He has been associated with other activists, like legal scholar Xu Zhiyong, who established Open Constitution Initiative, run from Beijing University, where he was an academic, with some funding from the Yale China Center, as a result of the iniquitous beating to death of a student in Guangzhou in 2003. Li's *Time* profile of 2004 refers to his involvement with supporting farmers standing in village elections in order to address local corruption and inequality. In an article for *Time* a year later, Li wrote that unrest had increased in China partly due to the increasing divide between rich and poor, but more pressingly because of 'the farmer's sense of powerlessness'. 'The central government has promised reforms that would give farmers more control over their lives. Those promises have been broken by corrupt local officials bent on keeping power and wealth for themselves.' Li concludes by asking, 'as unrest continues to mount, how long will Beijing be able to strike this balance [support for local officials with protection of the legitimate interests of common people] without real political reform?'

These profiles were written in the early period of the Hu-Wen leadership. They refer to newly ascended Hu as 'unlike his more aloof predecessor', a leader who 'has generally shown himself to be more accessible than any Chinese leader of the modern era'. As the only negative point, Li refers in the article to having had his website temporarily closed down, and being investigated by the secret police after one incident but thereafter being left alone. But six years on, this honeymoon era is long over.

In the summer of 2009 Xu Zhiyong, Li's protégé, was detained by Beijing city authorities, ostensibly over non-payment of taxes. In fact there was widespread speculation that he had fallen foul of the government and Party because of work he had been doing on Tibet and on open access to information. His source of funding from abroad was also seen as a problem. After a worrying few weeks he was set free, but the Open Constitution (*Gong Meng*) website was closed down for good. In a conversation with Li Fan while this was happening, he stated that at the 2008 'celebration' of the ten years of the Organic Law on Village Elections held in Beijing, many had stated that 'this was more like going to a funeral'. Hu Jintao had certainly not turned out to be a closet liberal, whatever the hopes held by some in the 1990s as he was preparing to become president and Party secretary. As the noughties decade wore on, it was clear that Hu was becoming even more repressive than his predecessor.

Li issues annual reports on the status of 'primary level democracy' in China. The report for 2009 states that due to the severe winter and all the problems it had caused in early 2008 (causing millions of migrant workers to be stranded during the major Spring Festival exodus back to home villages), the Wenchuan earthquake which killed tens of thousands in the middle of the year in Sichuan, and the Olympics in August, it had proved to be a momentous year. It had been, as Li stated, a year of volunteerism, of people willingly offering their help in the relief effort in Wenchuan, and at the Olympics. NGOs had become increasingly prominent, and the Internet had, at least momentarily during the Olympics itself, been opened up, linking even greater numbers of Chinese. The holding of government to account with the Open Government Information Act, which functions much like the Freedom of Information Act in the UK, had started to kick in. 'Dialogue between society and government had deepened', Li wrote.[30] But by the end of 2009, NGOs were suffering further restrictions, with many activists leaving (Wang Yanhai of the Aids group Aizhixing departed to the UK with his family in March 2010 citing police persecution), Google shifted its search engine from mainland China to Hong Kong to stop the censoring of results, and a raft of dissidents and activists were jailed or put under surveillance. The Shanghai Expo had seen over 6,000 'socially undesirables' rounded up and either removed from the city or told not to leave their homes. The Hu era had not been straightforward, as Mr Li was the first to admit.

Li was more than happy to admit this complexity. The first decade of village democracy had been good, he stated, but the second decade had been less easy. The townships had become increasingly keen on controlling the outcomes of village elections in their districts. There was too much at stake. In some places there had been out-and-out battles for control of the village chief position between the authorities and private business people. In others violence broke out almost as soon as elections were attempted. Anger ran high. Li had advised one man standing for the chief position not to get involved in punch-ups, by at least ensuring that there were bodyguards around him so if a scuffle broke out he wouldn't be the one carted off to jail. Unfortunately, Li sighed, the man had such a bad temper that the moment an argument flared up he had lashed out not only at his opponents, but at the people around him who were there for his protection. Police, Li admitted, just wanted the whole situation to blow over. It was a distraction for them and an unwanted expense to have to take someone off to jail for a few days.

Li's tracking of elections across the whole country has resulted in a stream of literature, reports and analysis. He has a small team with him in his office. He takes on these trips copies of his book, *Chinese Democracy in China*, giving it to officials and village leaders to read, so that they can learn the benefits of accountable government. Some provinces had been more successful than others. Guangxi, Liaoning, Jilin and Yunnan showed good progress, in his view. But the reports on central provinces of Hubei, Hebei, Henan and Hunan were less positive. This matches up with other indicators. According to a Hong Kong-based human rights analyst, these central 'H' provinces have the worst record for human rights abuses, the majority of petitioners originate from them, and they have some of the highest-profile instances of corruption. Henan, for example, suffered from the dreadful AIDS-contaminated blood scandal in the late 1990s, at the time when current vice premier and likely future premier Li Keqiang was Party boss there. As the *Guardian*'s Jonathan Watts writes in his study of China's environment, Henan, at only twice the size of Scotland, has a population of over 100 million people.[31] It is a province towards which people in the rest of China harbour prejudice and dislike. A friend in Beijing in 2008 told me the story of how former Premier Zhu Rongji in the 1990s had met with a man at a meeting in Beijing who stated he was the Party secretary of a region in Henan province famous for counterfeiting goods. Zhu had quipped 'So are you the real leader, or a fake one?' Another commentator, however, stated that the 'H' provinces were the places where social indicators were all reaching a critical level. There is a growing middle class, whose members are aware of their rights, and starting to use the courts, along with all manner of new forces in society unleashed by economic development. It is not surprising in view of this that resolving contentious issues in these places usually results in a great deal of fractiousness, and there are visible signs of discontent. As a sign of how challenging the governance of these places is, the Party Secretary of Hunan, Zhou Qiang, and other leaders of the central provinces, are often talked of as possible sixth-generation leaders, as long as they manage to control things in the difficult provinces where they are based.

Before we departed his small office, Li referred to the crisis in the final years of the noughties of public trust in government. Citing a celebrated annual survey in the magazine *Xiaokang* (Chinese for 'Moderate Prosperity'), published in China in 2009, Li pointed out that farmers were the most trusted in society, religious figures the second most trusted, and sex workers the third! Local government officials were by far the least trusted, coming in a little below national government figures. 'The problem is that over the last few years, trust in central government figures has fallen dramatically. It used to be that people put leaders in Beijing on a pedestal, and said they could sort things out. But that has been eroded. They are coming closer and closer to the same levels of distrust in which local officials are held.'

Referring to a famous case a few years previously, Li mentioned the disastrous impact that a farmer's wife had had when she managed to thrust her petition directly into the hands of Premier Wen Jiabao when in Beijing. (This faith that if the central leaders knew what the real situation was like on the ground they would intervene has deep historical roots in China. The practice of petitioning the emperor existed for centuries prior to being resurrected in the last decades under communism. Innumerable disillusioned officials and citizens wrote letters to Mao Zedong and Zhou Enlai begging for their intercession during periods of vicious social turbulence like the

Great Leap Forward, the Anti-Rightist Campaigns and the Cultural Revolution. Similar faith in the leader was manifested in the USSR during the Great Terror in the 1930s.[32]) The net result of this woman's penetration of Wen's security detail was that thereafter he was surrounded by even more heavies, and that people who subsequently met him were screened even more thoroughly beforehand.

When we left Li's office to walk into the rain which was just starting to fall, he shook my hand. 'Village elections have played their historic role', he said. He had stated in *Time* in 2004 that his big hope was that by 2020 China's president would be directly elected. Six years on, I did not dare ask him whether he still held this lofty aspiration.[33]

4

The great debate: where is Chinese
village democracy going?

This chapter will address three issues. It will do so largely through
the voices of Chinese people directly involved in the whole process
of village elections and democratic and governance reform in China.
The first issue is that of competitiveness. Are village elections, as
they now stand, truly competitive? Second, what are the views of
Chinese themselves about how the elections have gone? I will consider representative perspectives from activists, academic observers,
officials and intellectuals. Finally, I will look at the attempts made so
far to extend village elections to the township level, and beyond. The
key question is, in what way are these elections a stepping stone to
something more, and in what way are they purely a holding attempt
by the Party with no intention of expanding their reach? In the final
chapter, I will look at elections in the broader context of political
change within China in the future.

Competitiveness

There have been some very negative comments on the ability of
China to practise any form of democracy. Take American academic
Steven Mosher:

There is no Chinese tradition of respect for human rights, indeed no notion of inalienable rights at all. There is no ghost of a suggestion that Chinese government in any ways derives its just powers from the consent of the governed. From the beginning of Chinese recorded history, the emperor has been an absolute despot. In this regard, there is little to distinguish Qin Shihuang, who ruled from 221–206 BC, and Mao Zedong who ruled from AD 1949 to 1975 [*sic*], China's autocratic traditions provided no roots, and precious little foothold, for the foreign shoots of democracy.[1]

To cast such a huge net across all of recorded history in the area covered by the current PRC raises more questions than it answers. But this conviction that Chinese are somehow culturally, politically and even socially unable to practise democracy is surprisingly widespread, more often than not as much within the PRC as outside it. The key question, having acknowledged that village elections have taken place over the last two decades in China, is for us to ask in what sense are the elections genuinely competitive? And at the heart of this problem is the issue of believing that there can be decent elections without multiple parties. This is the usual characteristic of elections in Europe, North America and other areas with liberal democracies. Can China create democracy, but with one party in power?

In his study of rural democracy, Baogang He divides views on where elections fall between 'non-competitive' and 'semi-competitive'. The key issue is whether there is a choice, and what kind of choice there is, between candidates that stand for Village Committees. A single candidate stood in most elections in the early 1990s. From 1994, He states, multiple candidates have become the norm.[2] Surveys in the late 1990s showed that up to 70 per cent of all elections had a choice of candidate. Indeed, in some places subsequently so many candidates stood that it became quite tough to win the 50 per cent plus majority to get elected. With the appearance of multiple candidates came the need to campaign (*jinxuan*) so that those competing could set out their offers to the electorate. But He says that this practice remains frowned upon, quoting the case of

Miao Liangxiang, in a village in the south-east coastal province of Fujian, who broadcast his speech on village television, and was promptly rewarded with a 10,000 yuan (US$1,464) fine!³ Formal campaigns have been increasingly tolerated, and even encouraged, with candidates making speeches. But the appearance of multiple candidates and something approaching proper competition has also brought with it the less edifying phenomenon of vote-buying. Officials distinguish between legitimate canvassing for votes (called *labiao*, literally 'pulling votes') and illegitimate means (*maibiao*, meaning 'buying votes'). This is illegal, of course, but hard to prevent. In the new dynamic China where there is now a class of independently wealthy individuals, there is 'a competition of wealth: whoever can afford it, whoever spends the most, wins'.⁴ Gifts are given, dinners held, and a number of other inducements offered to secure villagers' votes. And while He argues that the wealthier areas see the most competitive elections (a suggestion others dispute), it is true that the land purchase and control powers of the Village Committee are attractive enough now to gain the interest of those wanting to make money, rather than just provide public service.

There are other issues that impact on just how competitive village elections can be. Kinship, mentioned in the last chapter, leads to family clans voting in blocs for each other. Ethnic blocs also exist. But as He finally admits, 'one significant feature of the village elections is the absence of multiparty competition.' There is no lack of candidates most of the time, but they cannot stand on any platform other than a CCP or non-Party-member one. In China 'the Party's dominance determines the extent of competition allowed and shapes the way the competition is conducted.'⁵ This often manifests itself in the control the Party has over the nomination process. Those who the Party branch does not favour locally it can simply refuse to nominate; or it can disrupt the process of those wishing to stand so much that it is impossible for them to proceed. For township leaders, electoral competition offers many potential threats. For instance, it could aggravate factional disputes, creating instability; or villagers might elect people who are regarded as unsuitable by township officials. Finally, competitive elections offer the possibility of loss of control. And to the CCP, loss of control, on whatever level, is what it most fears.

2009: a year of no significance

In a celebrated history of the Ming Dynasty (1367–1644), Ray Huang wrote about *1587: A Year of No Significance*. In the introduction to the book he says,

> Really, nothing of great significance happened in 1587, the Year of the Pig. China was not facing a foreign invasion, nor was the country engulfed in a civil war. ... On the whole, the Year of the Pig would go down in history as an indifferent one.

Nevertheless, the 'seemingly unimportant events' that took place in Ming China that year 'were closely linked to both her past and her future'. While nothing stood out in isolation as an epoch-breaking event, 'these interlinking events made history'. It is 'those commonplace occurrences which historians have been inclined to overlook that often reflected the true character of our empire'.[6]

As Li Fan noted, 2008 was a year of significance for a number of reasons: the hosting of the Beijing Olympics, the huge earthquake in Wenchuan, the terrible weather over the Chinese New Year, and (though he doesn't mention it) the explosion of protest and violence in Tibet, the worst for over half a century, in the spring. Compared to this, 2009 was relatively quiet. The only large event was the Xinjiang protests in July – but these were on a much smaller scale than the Tibetan ones had been. 2009 can therefore be described as 'a year of no significance' – but also a year in which, in retrospect, small, seemingly insignificant events at the time were ultimately to serve as portents of a deep, and cataclysmic, malaise. The regime was to collapse half a century later.

During this year of no significance, I spent the summer talking in Beijing, Shanghai, Hong Kong, and other centres, about China's political future with a group of academics, intellectuals, officials, Party members, NGO activists and foreign experts. The day on which I had arrived in Beijing had not been good. Xu Zhiyong, head of Open Constitution Initiative, one of the most liberal NGOs, had been detained. Over fifty lawyers had had their licences to practice law suspended, largely, it was thought, because they had defended sensitive cases like Falun Gong practitioners or property rights protesters. The famous dissident Liu Xiaobo remained detained, under house arrest (though he certainly wasn't at his home; no one knew quite where he was) for his involvement in the Charter 08 letter issued at the end of the previous year. Gao Zhisheng, one of the country's most prominent activist lawyers, who had been detained and tortured by police in 2007, had once more gone missing, earlier in the year (his case is discussed in the next chapter). Nothing had been heard of him for over six months. Meeting with one leader of a foreign organisation based in Beijing, he simply greeted me with the words 'You could not be here at a worse time' as I came through the door.

The best way to capture the conflicts and contradictions is to record summaries of conversations I had with people over this month-long period. I have grouped these into intellectuals and academics, practitioners, officials and outsiders. I have also concealed any indication of the identity of those speaking, in order to avoid any repercussions. This simple selection of viewpoints offers just a taster of the rich complex of ideas, perspectives and conflicts in China, most of it about the simple issue of village democracy and how that might relate to the governance of China as a whole in the coming decades.

THE EXPERT

Dr Tu has followed village elections for over fifteen years, and is compiling a huge database of their results – who stood, what they have achieved, how long they served, and so forth. 'After two decades, it is time to make a comprehensive assessment of where elections have come to', he says. To do this, he has divided the whole of China into five areas: the municipal areas of Beijing, Shanghai and Tianjin; the north-east provinces, of which there are three; the eastern provinces, of which there are seven; the central provinces, of which there are six; and the western provinces, covering vast swathes of the country and including ten provinces and five autonomous regions. Very broadly, he says, the pattern seems to be that developed and undeveloped places are not that interested in elections. The rich areas let business people buy votes, and the poor areas are too impoverished to find much value in ballots. But the middle areas are the ones that see the keenest, best-run elections. They have high voter turnout, with more than 93 per cent participating. In all areas, his research has shown that even asking voters to take time off from their work in order to cast their vote is difficult. It means loss of revenue. People are too busy making money to take time out to do something with no immediate economic benefit like this. He says:

> We now need to develop elections more quickly, but China is too big. How can you guarantee elections across such a vast, complex country that are uniform, and uniformly administered? And there is the problem of tradition. Local people always choose locals, and won't accept outsiders, even when they are better qualified to lead. For local elections there are many differences in administrative abilities, efficiency, even funding. Lack of education means that the talented people who succeed in getting voted in tend to move on quickly, headhunted by township governments. China's country-side has the same brain-drain problem as other impoverished areas.

China's electoral model, Dr Tu observes, is unique to itself. The question now is how to complete this model, how to choose officials efficiently who are qualified and best able to do their job. People's hopes regarding the impact of village democracy and the extension of democracy in other areas were sometimes pitched far too high. One thing was certain: village elections could not interrupt the work of the Communist Party of China. Only if democracy was conducive to good law-making and able to complement the leadership of the CCP could they continue. And, Dr Tu emphasised, if democracy inflamed separatism in places like Tibet or Xinjiang, then it was too dangerous to continue it. National unity was the most important factor. The CCP does not like risk; it wants gradualism and peaceful transition. There is a history of turbulence in China, from the Qing Dynasty onwards. Confucian hierarchy was also an impediment. 'We have fought against that', Dr Tu says, 'but the CCP cannot risk losing power. How can a Marxist people's government lose the support of the people?' Western cultures can tolerate individualism, he says, but in Eastern cultures the emphasis is on collective authority and consensus. The main issue is to prevent the overconcentration of power in the hands of a few. The greatest threat from popular plebiscites is to allow 'extreme nationalism'. 'Westerners who are always urging China to adopt a Western style of democracy need to remember that – they might end up with a government far more difficult to deal with, far more truculent, and far more aggressive than the Communists.' China needs to study foreign methods, according to Tu, but only use those that are appropriate for its own needs in the end. Citizen consciousness is low in the PRC, and is only just being created, and the experience of democracy in the USSR has shown that chaos and poverty can ensue, as they did in the 1990s after the fall of the Soviet state and the break up of the Union. That is something the PRC cannot and will not accept.

THE RETIRED OFFICIAL

Mr Wu is enjoying his retirement after more than forty years working in central government. He is to the point:

> There is no Chinese model. All that talk about a Chinese model is tosh. We just look around and see what suits the conditions of the moment here best. We are very pragmatic. Mr Deng Xiaoping was very pragmatic. We've had quite enough in the last few decades of dogmatism. Mao Zedong was always dogmatic, thinking there was some kind of science of social development. That is not true. We

look at experience. We can always learn things from elsewhere. We looked at what the Japanese did in their economy and legal system, and we copied parts of it. We looked at the German model too, and the US bicameral model. Since the global financial crisis from 2008, we have been much less keen to follow some kind of Western absolute path. Westerners need to be a bit more modest. They don't always have the right answers. Less and less these days, in fact. I met the prime minister of Singapore twelve years ago in Suzhou. He said that we had to follow the authoritarian system. Maybe that is what we have mostly done in the last few years.

But there are all sorts of things where we have had to innovate. Village elections were one of them. I think the idea came way back from what the USSR tried to do, but that was overtaken years ago. We had the commune system in the countryside until the 1980s; tremendously unproductive, it caused nothing but trouble. Once that was gone, there was a vacuum. So the pragmatic leadership in the 1980s thought of something to fill the gap quickly, and make sure that the rural areas didn't explode in riots and protests. They loosened up their economic structure so that farmers could sell surpluses back to the state and make money, and they allowed the establishment of enterprises once the productivity had improved. That had a huge impact. We went from being a food importer to being a food exporter. Of course, since then, things have changed, and we are starting to import food again – but that is because people have become choosy and want more meat and exotic stuff. It is unbelievable, isn't it, that in the 1960s we were still exporting grain to make money when our own people were starving? There is despotism for you. Thank goodness those days are over. No government we had would dare do that in the face of the people now. They really have to listen to public opinion, and try to reflect it in their policymaking. That was what I was doing for years in the central government.

Our system can live with contradictions. Look at the Land Contract Law in 2002 and the Village Law in 2001. One put a three-year limit on absent villagers being able to sublet their land while they were away elsewhere working. The other gave the Village Committee the power to reallocate land after a person had been away five years. It is the latter which now takes precedence. Even a law like this can cause problems. So the rightists say that we should follow the Land Contract Law, because it makes land easier to buy and sell by setting a shorter time limit. But the leftists say that we need to follow the Village Law because the land still belongs to the state, no matter what leases are used on it, and they want longer time limits for stability. Landowner rights in China are complicated anyway. In the past there were the real owners, the freehold owners as they are called in the West, and the rentiers. Now we say the state has freehold over every inch of land in China, but the rentiers are the people with various levels of leases. The Village Committees act as the agents for the state, via the communes. Legally, these still exist. Every five years, therefore, they have the right to redistribute land. That means that these village elections are meaningful. They confer real powers on the victors.

If they were totally meaningless, there would not be so much contention round them. When migrant workers go away, they subcontract their land. But these laws, however contradictory, make it clear that they can only do this for a limited time. And in law it is only the head of the Village Committee who can decide land contracts, not the Party branch secretary.

For Mr Wu, the greatest problem is corruption – the buying of power via committee elections. 'It is far worse than nationalism', he says.

To deal with corruption, there is only one way: to shine the light of scrutiny into the operations of government at whatever level. This is where we can and should copy the West. We need to put as much effort as possible into making officials accountable for the money they spend, how they spend it, and what they do. We need a transparent system of deciding property contracts in villages, rather than fixing things behind closed doors through personal connections. We need elections to be more representative of the communities they take place in. Democracy, when it works, roots out corrupt officials and wastage. In some villages where there have been good, properly competitive elections, you can see the difference the moment you walk in. The physical state of the village is better. It has useable public facilities. The living environment is good. That is where village democracy shows it is worth it.

Professor Dai has written a paper describing the Communist Party's attitude to democracy as like that of two people slowly falling in love before they get married. 'It has to grow and mature. Both sides need to feel comfortable with things. That is the natural process.' Regarding village elections, he is clear that the problem at the moment is that there are no immediate plans for their expansion beyond rural China. Democracy, he says, means many different things to different people. But so far, to be honest, Chinese leaders at the top have no clear goal. They have not thought through what they are going to do with this whole process. Some of them, like current premier Wen Jiabao, imply by a lot of their talk that they do want to see democracy progressed and taken forward. But others, like the more hardline number two in the Politburo, Wu Banguo, are far more cautious. The shadow of the elemental divide between rightists and leftists continues. What the leaders want most is a meritocracy. That is what people believe in. A system, any system, that promotes competent people. And the one thing they don't want is a system that offers any kind of threat to the monopoly of power of the CCP. 'The future', he says, holding his tea cup in a coffee shop by the entrance of the university where he teaches, 'is for China to be a consultative democracy'.

This would be a new model. The CCP would control the appointment of personnel, but the policies it implemented would in many cases be the result of extensive discussion with society. And the West, he says, 'needs to keep up the pressure on China to change. The PRC has signed international conventions on rights, it has revoked lawyers' contracts (see next chapter), and the West has barely said a word.'

'The government', Professor Dai says, 'would not do this if it thought there would be pressure from abroad. It should be held to the responsibilities it has signed up to. And embarrassed into behaving correctly sometimes.' This is particularly true in the case of NGOs, which still lack a clear legal status. This needs to be remedied, Professor Dai believes. 'There are now thousands of these groups, and they are all in a legal limbo.' Migrant workers remain disenfranchised.

> Sure, they can vote in the elections held in places where they come from, but how will that help them when they are based sometimes thousands of miles away working in cities or towns they are wholly strangers in? They have no rights, no residency permission, they live in a twilight world.

He admits things have got better over the last few years for migrant workers. But there are still too many restrictions. They lack the right to health care and to education for their children if they take these with them. And there is a high level of discrimination against migrants, with them suffering the classic stigma of all outsiders in being blamed for crime and social problems wherever they go. 'Foreign governments should put pressure on China', Professor Dai repeats, 'but they have to be very specific. And they shouldn't get drawn into issues about China's national territorial integrity. This will only cause confrontation. Secession is not a human rights issue.'

'Village elections', he says, 'have delivered accountability, this is true. Villages are able to send people to the higher levels of congress to participate in some decision-making. While the central government funds capital projects in villages, the Village Committee has powers over other budget lines. This is an important power.'

Dai admits with a shrug,

> Of course, there is corruption. Where isn't there corruption? But on the whole it works. Villages have become wealthier, the central government has reduced their tax burden. You even get villagers fighting to go back to their homes after years as migrants in order to reclaim their land, because it is so valuable. There is a gradually increasing reverse flow between the cities and the countryside.

Dai has made a specific study of what impact elections have had on the efficient expenditure of money. 'It is incontrovertible. Elected Village Committees reduce public expenditure. Income distribution also improves. They are better at looking after the poor. They invest more in education and public utilities.'

Where has village democracy worked best? I ask. In the richer or poorer areas? Or the middle areas? Without hesitation, he says 'Coastal regions. Wealthy regions. If you want to be a village head in Yunnan, where is the gain? But where average income is higher, people see the value in voting. They want to participate.' And then he adds, 'Village elections have a huge impact on democratisation. They show democracy can work. You shouldn't underestimate the meaning of that.' Even if multiparty elections are not possible? 'People can represent themselves, and stand independently.' He thinks for a while. 'The government, over the last thirty years, has been willing to cede economic rights to people. But not political rights.' Its greatest immediate challenge? I ask. 'How to act with more transparency', he says.

> Look at the way we pass our national budget. All tax revenues go to the central state for redistribution. Can you imagine how complex our national budget is? Trillions of Chinese yuan, over hundreds of pages. We have one of the largest economies in the world. And yet, every year when the budget comes up for discussion at the NPC, it gets delivered the night before to the delegates in their hotel rooms, and then has to be discussed and passed before noon the next morning.

Only a few days after meeting with Professor Dai, I noticed that the whole budget of one of China's wealthiest and largest provinces, Guangdong, had been put online. The file came in at 2 gigabytes. Someone who tried to download it found that it flooded the entire storage capacity of their computer. But it was a major step forward. Perhaps Professor Dai is right, and one day the CCP will be able to live with transparency.

THE THINKER

Mr Bo gives me his latest book, signing it carefully before handing it over. 'Not easy to get hold of, these days', he says. 'Sold far better than I thought.' We get down to business.

> Village elections were not imposed from above. They were a natural product of the desires of the people in rural China, a response to the years in which they suffered poor and unstable rule. Some aspects of the elections were taken from abroad: the secret ballot, and then the multiple candidates. We did have some historical memory. You have probably heard of the Yan'an elections, where they used bean counters, in the 1940s, when the Communists were based there.[7] Most of their followers were from the poorest areas of the countryside, so there were high levels of illiteracy. Elections don't just belong to the West. They are part of our heritage too.

He looks at me meaningfully. And how would he assess the current situation? 'Wealthy areas have produced issues', he says;

> the middle and poorer areas are OK, but where you get newly emerging elites, they try to challenge the authority of everyone for their own business purposes. Of course in the early 2000s we thought we had dealt with this by allowing entrepreneurs into the Party again. We started giving business people a bigger voice. But in the end, their objective is to make money. As you have also discovered in the West in this terrible financial crisis, if you don't give people a legal structure to work in, then they take liberties. We have found whole areas of the countryside being dominated by mafia – particularly in the north-east, and then in the coastal areas down south. Triads from Hong Kong and Russian gangsters, who are funding their business partners to then get elected, and before you know it they have stitched up whole areas of the countryside, running it like a personal company.

He lights a cigarette, blowing smoke over me and his assistant, who sits silently beside him. It is about eleven in the morning, and the street outside is oddly quiet. 'The concept of freedom', he says, 'is one that we have, very strongly.'

Our elections are free, freer than in the West, freer than in the
United States. There are no parties. People stand for themselves.
So, in some senses, they are too free. There are no restrictions and
restraints on what you can say. You have five people stand, you
have five totally different perspectives. You have ten people, then
you get ten perspectives. It's something that people have criticised.
They end up a lot of the time as a total free-for-all. At least political
parties would rein people in and discipline them a bit. This is why
the more conservative elements of the Party argue that the whole
election process, including who stands, should be put under the
Party branch. If you give the Village Committee too much power,
then it is easy for it to become corrupt. So the conservatives also
say that now they have to be scaled back, and that they are causing
more harm than good. This is a big debate in the Party.

'But the main opinion', Mr Bo says, after a short pause, while he
thinks, looking at the table, 'is that they have to continue'.

The conservatives have won one concession. In the upper levels
of the Party there is an understanding now that the choice of
candidates has to be controlled. If victors in elections can't deliver,
then the townships or above have to get rid of them, even if their
time is not yet up. The gold standard is development. This is
in accordance with Party Secretary Hu Jintao's idea of scientific
development. Where villages develop and deliver prosperity and
measurable improvements in the services for their people, then we
can say that the right people are in charge, and they will be left to
carry on their work. We have agreement now that we cannot allow
village committees to become overpowerful and run their areas like
private fiefdoms. So some government interference is necessary.

Control over budgets and money, he says, is always where the power
is:

This is where Village Committees have to be held accountable.
This is now an area of active debate within government. And to
hold these officials to account, we need to have a better means of
representation. The basic idea is that village congresses are the
parliament. Every fifteen households have one representative. That

is ridiculously high. If a parliament is going to work, it needs far fewer representatives. We can't try and govern by listening to the views of everyone. That way, we'd never get anything done. We need to find a means of filtering out bad ideas and keeping in the good ideas. So a better means of running congresses is important, and making them more representative. Then we need to sort out where different responsibilities lie. They are doing some interesting things in Chengdu, Sichuan, over in the south-west – actually holding competitive elections for the village congress, too, and reducing its size.

There is another long pause, then Mr Bo continues with his theme.

Accountability is the biggest issue. That is the way you discipline democracy. In Henan, they have a three votes system. Democracy doesn't just end when you cast your vote for who will sit on the Village Committee. At the end of the first year there is a survey. People are asked, are you satisfied with the leaders, are you satisfied with the Party branch, and are you satisfied with the township governance over your own village? If the satisfaction rate is below 80 per cent, then there are consequences, and these become particularly severe if it falls below 50 per cent. Leaders that fail to reach 80 per cent have to appear before committees to explain themselves. Under 50 per cent, and you have to resign. In Zhejiang province, they have created a Discipline and Inspection Committee overseeing finances. The inspection of finances, of where money is spent and how, is absolutely key.

And Party accountability? I ask. Where does the Party come in all of this?

Of course the powers of the Party branch secretary are large and wide-ranging. It is contradictory to have one part of the local government accountable to elections and processes of scrutiny, and have another wholly opaque. One solution is to make Village Committees and the Party work in unison. Party people have to engage in village elections. So there is the two votes idea, where the villagers choose a candidate for Party branch secretary, and then the Party approves this. There should be political competition, at least to be Party branch secretary. In Sichuan, again, we have innovation. Party members directly choose members of the Party committee. Internal Party competition is good. The Party needs to improve its technical ability, its ability to govern efficiently and within its resources.

'The key thing', and here Mr Bo speaks slowly and very deliberately, 'is to create consensus. Ours is a system that must create consensus.'

We are winding up. I have already put away my notepad and pen. Mr Bo is standing, ready to go. Almost as an afterthought, he mentions Charter 08, the demand for greater democracy and rights issued after the Olympics, which had seen some of its main signatories put in jail.

> There is no problem with putting ideas out there, and, sure, there were many ideas on that document that we wouldn't have a major problem with. We are in the midst of a huge debate. There are all sorts of idea we are looking at. But the main issue with the Charter 08 group is that they don't say clearly what their objective is. What were they really after? Why did they do what they did? They have an ulterior motive, which they have hidden. The Party can't tolerate that. It is a direct challenge to its legitimacy.

Only a few months later, on Christmas day 2009, the main protagonist behind the drafting of the Charter 08 document, Liu Xiaobo, was imprisoned for eleven years. It was the harshest sentence yet given under the anti-subversion law introduced in 1998.

THE FOREIGN OBSERVER

> It all gets complicated the moment you mention democracy, what people mean by democracy. Freedom House, an American think-tank that monitors countries for levels of openness and democracy, ranks China very low in terms of the freedom and accountability of its systems and public institutions. Of course, there has been a huge change since 1979. It is a different country now to the way it was then. The government is much more responsive to people's needs. In looking at villages that have held elections, there are

two types. Those in which the whole election process and the institutions of Village Committees and congresses have grown out of traditions and those where they are a wholly new phenomenon. Of course, this has a big impact on how successful or not they have been. Foreign assistance was very important early on. The EU, the Ford Foundation and the United Nations Development Programme (UNDP) all gave money to the Ministry of Civil Affairs to help it develop elections. The main impact of all this at least created a group of reform-minded officials, and without their support and patronage nothing would have been achieved. One of them was so important in the Ministry of Civil Affairs that he got the nickname 'Mr Democracy'. But, for some reason, in the early 2000s he was moved on, and in fact from that time the whole process lost a lot of its momentum.

How you measure change is a big problem. It is never going to be easy to do that, which is why the outcomes of such a massive process as village elections is still so contentious. No one can really easily agree because you can't stand back from such a dynamic process and say, at any one moment, this is where we really are. The moment you do so, things have already moved on. On the relationship between the Communist Party and elected officials there will always be competition. Whatever model, even if it is the 'carrying on one shoulder' or the two votes system, is not going to easily deal with this. In many places, whatever you like to say, there is a power struggle. There are no clear rules here. It is entirely dependent on the specific case. When conflict really gets out of hand, then the first step is for the township to intervene. Sometimes it works. Sometimes it doesn't.

In fact, Chinese leaders are very different to each other. Jiang Zemin, Party head and president from 1989 to 2002, was the Republican, supportive of business, trying to make for a less interventionist state. Hu Jintao has been a Democrat. He supports the grassroots and workers more, with the lifting of tax burdens on farmers and attempts to do something about creating more balanced, equal growth. Jiang supported the bourgeoisie; Hu supports the workers. Their whole political complexion is different. For the CCP the highest political premium is on survival. The CCP would willingly do anything to preserve itself in power. That is the only thing that matters in the end. It can make big adjustments. You can see it all the time in the way it behaves, introducing policies one minute people would have thought impossible only a little while before. Movements like Charter 08 are regarded with deep fear and dislike because there, in the heart of what they do, is an attempt to create organised opposition. For the CCP, its legitimacy is based on making China strong and prosperous. It argues that political opposition in the form of other parties would smash this, creating instability. It is the trump card it uses every time anyone or any organisation does something that seems to creep towards organised political opposition. At the moment, the CCP can't compromise over this. And when you look at the little evidence there is in surveys that have been done on the public, support for the CCP is high. Foreigners who want to see China democratise need to think carefully about this. They shouldn't just daydream. The CCP is broadly supported by the people. Oddly enough, in China the more educated someone is, the less they trust the government. In other countries, it is usually the other way around.

Data. The key thing that will always be needed is data: about what is happening, what people are thinking, what they are doing. The more data the better. And then the right tools to disaggregate it and interpret it and make sense of it.

THE CONTRARIAN

Professor Tang is surrounded by students when I manage to track him down in a tea shop in the north of Beijing. He is not an easy man to get hold of. Calls to his mobile phone largely go unanswered. Emails rarely get any reply. But finally, he is there – sitting in a corner, hunched over like a praying mantis about to strike. Village elections have made things worse, he says.

> Of course foreign funding is ideologically driven. That is why a number of famous activists were all supported in the past. But, honestly, where has it led to? Some parts of the country are in complete chaos: run by thugs and conmen, all after their own gain. These elections don't fit into the pattern or traditions of rural life in China. I have studied this. The major connection in all villages, and the major cause of divisions, is classes. Democracy tries to cut across this, setting people against each other.

He watches me as I write, as though waiting for a response.

> Chinese governance in villages is always by the minority. Democracy has caused perverse outcomes. The only way the Chinese government has been able to deal with this is to send outsiders in to stabilise and sort things out. That is the same principle the Party uses when it appoints provincial heads. Never allow the Party boss in a province to be a local. That way, all the old tribal allegiances start up. The provinces with locals in the top slots end up being run like mafia or small family businesses, full of corruption and lack of accountability. The majority principle is not one that leads to justice in Chinese villages. Ever since the 1980s, the CCP has tried to implement majority rule, through these elections and a whole raft of other measures, largely based on consultation. We need neutral, dispassionate government, a government that can sit back and sort out some of the contentions between different sections of society, not make them worse. The system of majority-led rule is not appropriate to China. There are too many divisions already. Letting the majority have the upper hand all the time just means pressure builds up, and one day... one day, there will be an explosion. Of course, this is very frustrating to the propagators of democracy in rural China, foreigners and Chinese. They really hate to see this kind of setback. But that is because they don't understand village life. I was born in a village. I lived until I was 15 in a village. I understand these places because it is where I am from, and it is in my bones and my DNA.

'Why do you think', he declares, addressing me as he would a public meeting, 'that the CCP has called a halt to elections?' 'Has it?' I ask, 'They still seem to be going on.' He looks at me as if I am unutterably naive.

> They go on, but purely as an outward show. If they had any meaning, the Ford Foundation and the Carter Center and the EU would still be supporting them. The CCP can't be bothered to axe them, so it just lets them carry on, and puts in real power structures all around them. For the last two decades, we have seen the basic infrastructure of governance in these villages eroded. Who knows what is really happening in some of these places? The collapse of

the CCP and the Party branch system have left places simply not functioning. Then the criminals and the hardmen come in and take over. Just like after the breakdown of governance in the USSR.

'That was the case in the 1970s, after the Cultural Revolution', I say. 'There was widespread chaos then. But surely elections were brought in to sort this out?' 'Nonsense', the professor says,

> village elections were brought in as a sop to the liberals, who were influential in the 1980s. They were motivated purely by ideology. But, in that sense, they have been very helpful. The fact that they have so signally failed just proves that all this stuff from intellectuals here about us needing to use more Western ideas is not right. Western ideas don't apply to the reality in China. That is what this vast failed experiment proves.

'Legal reform', he says, 'that is much more successful. We can do nothing without the rule of law. The rule of law assists the maintenance of stability in China, and helps in making people more prosperous. So, of course, the Party must support that.' His voice grows a little shriller again,

> But pro-Western activists are always opportunistic. So they have done their best to make this area one that is malleable to their own objectives. Lawyers are trained in that way here. They are made to ideologically oppose political intervention in legal affairs, and to challenge the CCP's legitimacy. Most of the main activists in China who oppose the CCP most strenuously come from a legal training background. Look at Charter 08. There it is in black and white. The majority of people who signed this were lawyers. So now the CCP sees lawyers as a threat, and they look at the way these lawyers have been funded. Much of it comes from the West. Many of these lawyers are practising a form of legalism that doesn't fit into reality in China. In China, human relationships, what we call *renqing*, are the most important thing.

'Isn't that reverse Orientalism?' I ask. Professor Tang goes almost puce with rage. 'This is the situation in China. We won't bear any more of the West, especially Europeans, coming over here to give us lectures on what we should and should not do, and adopting a position of' – here he slows down to an almost declamatory style – 'moral superiority'.

> We need to return to Chairman Mao's concept of democracy. We must absorb ideas from outside, for sure, but tradition must be our backbone. We need a new form of traditionalism in China. Tradition is the future. Even if the CCP were to fall tomorrow, a new elite would emerge; there is no space for parliamentary democracy here. People say Taiwan shows that Chinese can become democrats. That's rubbish. The Taiwanese Democratic Party represents the native Taiwanese. The Nationalist Party are the incomers. It's a purely tribal division. There is nothing ideological about it. Democratisation and competitive elections were supported by many people inside and outside China purely to overthrow the current system. That is all. Let us be honest. But they failed, OK, they failed. These enemies will try to find some other way to sneak their bad intentions in here. But the CCP's main legitimacy now is through reform, and that means it has to experiment sometimes. Don't interpret that as a sign of weakness.

Looking at me sharply, he says: 'It is, in fact, a sign of strength.'

THE SECURITY MAN

He has a smooth, silky voice and a smooth, silky manner. Nothing seems to perturb him. His handshake is firm, but soft. Relaying my conversation with Professor Tang, he laughs quietly. 'The new leftists are worse than the ones we had in the old times.' I ask him what China's current greatest challenge is. 'Economic reform', he says. 'And, of course, reform of the political and administrative system.' 'How?' I ask.

> The roots of Chinese democracy are not where you expect them to be. They are in the Cultural Revolution. At that time, there was lively, passionate debate within the whole of society. Sometimes it got out of hand. But, many times, it taught people of my generation the value of open debate. We were able to discuss anything

then. Lots of sacred cows were knocked down. We should not overinterpret conflict. Chinese know how to deal with conflict. We have had many centuries to deal with it. Foreigners shouldn't worry about things being too bad here. They should look at Russia, parts of Africa, North Korea [DPRK], even places in Latin America, and the Middle East. The problems there are far greater, the governments far less legitimate, and the possibilities of real implosion very great. Our government has delivered stable rule, and development. And we are still reforming. We won't stop doing that. Of course, in the village elections, we saw the problems early on of conflict between the Party and the elected heads. But we did things in a step-by-step way. We have managed the risk. The three greatest risks in the coming decade are clear. We have to continue with reform and development, and make development the first priority; that remains at the core of what we do. We must deal with our environmental and resource challenges, because they are becoming increasingly great, and we must deal with social instability. We know, from what others have been through, that when you hit per capita average incomes of from US$3,000 to 6,000, then you are in a potentially dangerous transition. That is when you have to think hardest about enfranchising a middle class. That is why we need to have thought through the best development model.

We are already dealing with an increasingly demanding population, so we need to embed the rule of law in everything we do. Property rights are a major problem, so we need to clarify those. We have looked hard at Western political models, especially the bicameral model, and concluded that they are not suitable. While economic reform has been going on, of course, we have been thinking too about the risks of not having proper political reform. We will start to make bigger steps here. We have to think about negative social outcomes, but we cannot be timid. The Communist Party is sitting on an enormous historical contradiction. It has its roots in illegality. The link between legality and legitimacy is not direct. Unity, stability, prosperity, these are more important than legality. But now the Party needs law, and this is why our president said during the unrest in Xinjiang in July this year [2009] that there has to be one law over the whole land. We can't have a different law for different places. The main requirements of the students in 1989 when they protested have been fulfilled, because China has continued to open up, to build a rule of law, and to maintain openness. Officials are accountable for their actions now.

Some foreigners are here to do things which lead to negative social effects. They are a direct challenge to our sovereignty and to the stable rule of the CCP. We have looked hard at the Colour Revolutions that happened after the USSR fell apart and concluded that foreign involvement there was very negative. It created problems which it was not then willing to handle responsibly once things deteriorated. It was a destructive element, not a positive one. Lawyers and NGOs were used as frontmen for this attack. This is why we must be wary. We must always be wary. Those who want to act according to the law, and in the spirit of supporting unity and stability, they are always free to do as they want, but those who harbour other motives, they must be dealt with. A government is here to deal with practical details, feeding, protecting, looking after its own people. It is not here to improve the consciousness of democracy.

Contention as the key link

This chapter has presented just a few voices from the great debate about China's future. There are many others, who have talked about the real problems of increasing violence in Chinese society, of the creeping and insidious influence of the security services, and of a range of other problems, some of which will be dealt with in the next chapter. Yet across the whole range of governance issues there seems little agreement. Here is a society engaged in profound change, and the one structure that is common to all of this is the role of the CCP and its dominance. Beyond this, there is next to no agreement.

The year 2009 saw no great events. China put no one on the moon. It was involved in no major wars. Its involvement in an international financial bailout was noteworthy, but would we really remember this in ten years time, or beyond? No major leaders rose or fell over the course of the year. In that sense, for the chronologists, it was truly a year of no significance. And yet, simple discussions like this, in various places around Beijing and elsewhere in China, in their own modest way, gave small clues to the ways in which the tectonic plates of this immense society were shifting. There were signs of immense impending change, and of societal decisions being slowly made. Perhaps fittingly, as I neared the end of my tour, an almighty thunderstorm in Beijing saw a deluge of rain sweep the usually dry August streets clean. There was an apocalyptic feel about the city that evening.

Mao Zedong famously called Chinese people 'a blank sheet of paper'. On this he wrote his highly idiosyncratic vision of a perfecting society, hurtling towards Utopia. The misery this caused turned the whole machinery of government and the state against its own people. Few speak seriously of any desire to return to the Maoist vision. The most they will say now is that at the very least corruption was under control then – though other hideous abuses of official power were all too common in those years. In another phrase, the other great dictator of the twentieth century for Chinese, Chiang Kai-shek, said the Chinese were like sand – impossible to gather in one place, or fit into one category.

For some Chinese, elections at the village level have brought improvements. For others, they have created greater instability and violence. The question remains, however, in what way can governance, accountability and transparency be supplied in a society undergoing such evident change? To start thinking about possible answers to this, it is now time to put village elections in the context of other areas of social change going on in Chinese society. Some of these have been alluded to by the speakers above – law, civil society and participation in governance. The final chapter will therefore put the whole electoral experience within this bigger picture.

5

The big picture: elections as part of the dynamics of a society in change

Chapter 2 stated that in the last decade Chinese society has been in ferment. This is a consequence of rapid economic and social change, huge processes of urbanisation, and the appearance of increasing numbers of migrant workers. It has been commonplace for commentators to say that China is trying to achieve in the space of a couple of decades what developed countries took over a century to do. The fault lines in Chinese society are easy enough to find. 'Unless China embarks on reform in its basic political system, its chances of achieving full-scale modernisation by the end of this century is next to zero', says a report by Professor He Chuanqi, director of the Centre for Modernisation Research at the Chinese Academy of Science, issued in January 2010. He blames China's huge population, regional imbalances, income disparity, resource depletion, environmental degradation and lagging political reform. 'Once weighting is assigned to each of these factors, one arrives at a very low probability [for modernisation]', he says.[1] There are plenty of other sobering voices.

One group of populist writers in the spring of 2009 decided to revisit an earlier success they had been involved in, a book titled *The China That Can Say No*. Led by writer and academic Wang Xiaodong, they issued a rousing corrective to the nascent nationalism that had appeared during the Beijing Olympics. In *China Is Not Happy* they set out the causes of their current discontent – a discontent, they argue, that is shared by most of the young in China.[2] A good deal of the book, which is divided into a number of separate short essays (including translations from Western media, and even a speech on China by former British prime minister Tony Blair), deals with the increasing frustration among some communities within China at the ways in which their country is perceived by the West and then treated in the international system. The Olympic torch ceremony through most of early 2008, with the fractious scenes that occurred in many places along its route, is taken as an event of high symbolic value. The West (which for much of the book is simply shorthand for the USA) is accused of 'obstruction', using the methods piloted during the Colour Revolutions in states that broke away from the former Soviet Union to control the PRC.[3] The PRC, in cooperation with the Western economic system, has become 'the factory of the world', allowing exploitation of cheap workers and major environmental degradation. While *China Is Not Happy* was presented in some parts of the Western media as a representative sample of angry, ugly Chinese nationalism, hitting out at the developed world, in fact a more careful reading shows that this was only the surface. The real culprits, in the eyes of the book's authors, were not outside, but within – the elites, who had led China into this miserable impasse. And while not mentioning the leadership of the CCP, it is clear that they are in Wang et al.'s sights.

This becomes clearer when speaking specifically about the milk powder scandal in 2008 that resulted in the deaths of many young babies. Huang Jilao states: 'Everyone can ask themselves, "manage", this word, right, means "manage" ... But for years, you've been poisoning us. So how is that 'managing'?[4] It is here that the authors' arguments become highly political. Issues of official complicity in incidents like this are why 'the common people need "democracy" and "freedom" to limit the powers of some officials', they argue.[5] The question is, however, whether the PRC currently has the capacity for democracy as it stands?[6] The PRC wishes, the authors state, to have a big objective – to be stable, peaceful and, less promisingly, 'to control more and more resources'.[7] The elites, however, in their attempts to pursue a big objective, have 'been eaten up by the West'. The West is accused by the authors of finding a modernising, industrialised and strengthened PRC 'unbearable'. A number of faintly paranoid schemes are envisaged where China is manipulated into conflict with Russia or Japan.[8] In order to build its capacity, 'first China must battle in the markets', and then 'prepare afterwards for military action, using our industrial basis as a foundation'.[9] Elites in China have allowed the West 'to exploit our cheap labour'.[10] The options are either 'to use war, or to let a big country like us continue to use the model of letting our people's blood and sweat support Western leadership'.[11] With the loss of moral authority on the part of the West after the George W. Bush presidency and its actions in Iraq from 2003 onwards, and the 2007–09 financial crisis, China now has an opportunity to lead.[12] But whether the world is ready to 'give us a chance to realise a modern democracy' is another matter.[13]

In this era of frustration at the complicity of the elites in global capitalism on a Western-led model, the possibilities of social explosion are very high.[14] New Confucianism, a recently created hybrid of Asian values, respect for tradition and order, and hierarchy, receives short shrift, leading to a 'country ruled solely by elites'. Instead,

> If history chooses for China to adopt Western-style democracy, I am fine with that. Put another way, if history reveals that the possibilities of China implementing a non-Western form of democracy are not strong, but that it is quite likely it can use a Western form of democracy, then that's cool. But regardless of what system is used, anything is better than a non-democratic system.[15]

So, while China can contemplate a 'conditional rupture' with the West, and look seriously at trade wars and other attritional conflicts in order to deal with the USA and others' attempts to contain and repress its national development, paradoxically the authors of *China Is Not Happy* are relaxed about importing from outside political models that might work in the PRC. Their real argument, beyond the USA, is with their own elites – the very elites whose restrained views are encapsulated in 'The Six Whys', discussed in Chapter 2.

China Is Not Happy does not engage with the issue of internal reform in any detail. The thrust of its argument is how the PRC constructs a suitable image of itself and is able to project respect and strength based on its newly established economic and political power. But the anger and frustration with elites (in Chinese, *jingying*) is clear throughout the various contributions. Crucially, though, these are not specifically named as the leaders of the CCP, who in many ways would be most guilty of the acts of collaboration that are detailed in the work.

The link between rural democracy and the complaints against elites in a populist work like *China Is Not Happy* might not seem that clear. But they are both part of an immense and increasingly passionate and wide debate within China about where the country is heading. At the heart of this is the political system that truly befits its status as a major international economy. And that involves talk, finally, about what system is best able to deliver good governance and allow people in both rural and urban China to feel enfranchised and able to participate in decision-making.

This final chapter will therefore reach out from the specific issue of rural democracy, which has been covered in the previous chapters, and look at the whole issue in the broader context of debate about political change in China generally. It will first of all look at the attempts that are guiding the current elite leadership of the CCP to be 'consultative' and 'place people at the centre'. The chapter will then deal in turn with the three great areas of reform: the legal system, NGOs and political participation. Each of these has come up in discussions above. Now they will be set together, to see where and how what has been happening in the countryside might have relevance in the cities and country as a whole.

Having a heart: the Hu era and consultative Leninism

Oxford academic Steve Tsang has argued that while 'communism effectively ceased being the state ideology in China some time between the Tiananmen protests of 1989 and the collapse of Communism in Eastern Europe and the Soviet Union in the following two years', it has maintained a Leninist political system.[16] In the social contract of the new China, 'the Party delivers stability, order, rapid growth, and general improvements to the living conditions of the people in return for its continuing dominance of government and politics.' 'The general improvement in living conditions', Tsang goes on to admit, 'includes not only economic prosperity, but a larger scope for individual freedom, and improved government responsiveness to public demands.'[17] And there, as they say, is the rub. More and more people, including academic Pan Wei, mentioned in Chapter 2, one of contemporary China's most prominent leftists, are talking of the need to move beyond just delivering economic indicators. But once out of that territory, things become a whole lot more complicated. 'China has indisputably been a factory for GDP growth in the last three decades', as one well-known businessman then based in Beijing commented to me in 2008. 'But when you look at measures beyond that, it is much less clear what has been achieved.' Some have grown wealthy, and yet there are as many as 24 million malnourished people, and 200 million still living in poverty. Some have been lifted into education, but the education system still fails many others in parts of rural or western China. And as the series of brutal stabbings[18] at schools across China in spring 2010 showed, there are plenty of people who are pushed to extreme measures by their anger at the system and the way it has dealt with them.

Part of the problem for observers has been simply to work out what sort of system we are dealing with. As far back as the seventeenth century, as a scholar from China commented at a talk in 2007 in London, foreign missionaries went to China and sent back confusing reports about what it was that Chinese people believed. They were not all Daoists, nor were they all Buddhists, or Confucianists. There were some Christians, and even a minority of Muslims and Jews. The question, 'What do Chinese believe?' is no easier to answer now than it was back then. There are indeed 76 million members of the CCP, and 84 million in its Youth League. But that accounts for a mere 14 per cent of the whole population. There are over 100 million Muslims, over 100 million Christians, and possibly as many as half a billion Buddhists. Daoists still exist. Spiritual sects like the Falun Gong continue to attract people, no matter how brutally outlawed they are. And in the cities, as a string of books and films made by Chinese have shown, a disenchanted nihilism reigns. As an academic noted in 2001, the 'post-Communist type-man' (the vast majority of Communist mid- to upper-level cadres are men) is light on beliefs, even while he lives in a society where ideology still seems on the surface to be important.[19] As China embarked on the great transformation in the 1980s, some wrestled with how best to describe the system it was developing. American academics Kenneth Lieberthal and David Lampton devised the term 'fragmented authoritarianism' in the 1980s.[20] This seemed to capture the constant tensions between the central state under communism, and the multiple localities of which contemporary China is made. As Oxford-based academic Vivienne Shue commented, 'Many givens of Chinese politics were decisively overturned when the Communist Party came to power, but the abiding tension between state-centre and locality was not one of these.'[21] Fragmented authoritarianism also referred to the ways in which large areas of economic and social life were freed up, but with core interests still protected by the supremacy of the CCP. In the 1990s there was more talk of a 'party state', where the CCP operated almost as its own 'state within a state', echoing comments made about the position the Communist Party was in during its years of subterfuge in the late 1920s by historian of the early years of the Party, Jerome Chen: 'the situation in July and August 1927 was inevitable – the CCP had to have an army, a territory, and a government. In other words, it had to make a state within a state.'[22] This resulted initially in the short-lived Jiangxi Soviet, established at the end of the 1920s, of which Mao was to serve as president. Increasingly, as it grew older, the Party-state returned to this model, almost working as a separate economy and entity, paralleling the structures of government and business and civil society, but somehow managing to embed itself in key strategic areas.

Leaders of the CCP wrestle as much as anyone else with what it is and what structures it can function with. Deng, Jiang and now Hu have tried to craft a new ideological take which will somehow spell out to people, inside and outside China, what the Party's vision is, and where it best fulfils its role. For Hu, the attempt has been much more to link with the very people who vote in village elections, with the grassroots. Despite his stiff and formal manner, he has been keen to present himself as a man of the people, putting service back at the heart of the government's agenda. In the terrible earthquakes in 2008 in Sichuan, and 2010 in Gansu, he and other key members of his government rushed to the scene of the disaster to show that they are in charge, and that they are responding. Hu and Wen have participated in Internet chats and discussions, and even, briefly, before it was blocked in China, had Facebook pages. At the Seventeenth Party Congress in 2007, Hu spoke of 'a people-centred socialism'. This accords with the amount of work spent on 'harmonious society' and 'scientific development', both buzzwords of the last few years, and, perhaps even more importantly, of social justice. Justice is the key issue in Hu's China, and the delivery of justice remains one of the top priorities. Beyond what one critic has described as a leadership based on rhetoric that hides a regime 'devoid of serious doctrines or views',[23] the key question is how to deliver through social infrastructure like courts, the legal system, civil society and the media outcomes which help with justice, but do not result in politically unacceptable outcomes – in this case the loss of a monopoly on political power by the CCP. This is the great conundrum being faced by the CCP elite leadership as they travel on into the twenty-first century.

Courts and the rule of law

Since 1978, the government of the PRC has recognised the importance of building a rules-based system by which to help its economic
growth and social development. Official historians have divided
post-1949 history into the period up to 1978 dominated by the 'rule
of man' (*ren zhi*), with the increasingly centralised power of Mao
Zedong, and the period of 'rule of law' (*fa zhi*), which has been the
great aspiration since then. In June 1949, a legal committee under the
CCP held a seminar with the Ministry of Justice, which, as a result,
drafted a criminal law in 1950. Despite discussion at the first NPC
in 1954, and over twenty-two separate drafts, political campaigns
like the Anti-Rightist Movement (1957) and the Cultural Revolution
(1966–76) meant that the proposal was never implemented. According to one scholar in Beijing, 'the whole of society put too much
emphasis on public security and order, with a very weak awareness
of individual rights... The understanding of rights protection was to
prevent the criminal being at large rather than protecting the rights
of the defendant.'[24] There was no private sector, no commercial law,
no contract or bankruptcy law, and no concept of property rights.
In the last three decades, the Communist Party has tolerated the
construction of a whole legal edifice, borrowing and adapting widely.
German laws and legal cooperation in the 1980s followed intense
work with Japan. Over 450 pieces of separate legislation have been
passed, with a new system, in which over a million lawyers have been
trained, in all areas of the law, and courts opened at the five main
levels of government, from the town up to the centre in Beijing.

This legal revolution was provoked not so much by principle as by
an acute awareness under the Deng leadership that without foreign
technology and assistance, China's aspirations to get on a fast track
to development were going to be hard, if not impossible, to fulfil.
China needed laws that first allowed, and then protected, foreign
enterprises coming to China. It needed instruments to protect investment, and to create joint-venture structures. It needed laws to

manage its own enterprises, with contracts, bankruptcy and tax. Most importantly, it needed the rule of law to stabilise society after the widespread chaos of the Cultural Revolution and the twilight years of the Maoist era. This whole process was successful enough to mean that by the 1990s China was one of the world's largest recipients of inward investment, with a stock at the end of 2009 of almost US$700 billion.

Entry to the WTO prompted a second wave of commercial law reform in 2001, with many of China's laws in this area harmonised with the responsibilities it had undertaken on joining the organisation. By 2006, it had, on time, implemented all of the major provisions and commitments it had made under its WTO agreement, at national and provincial levels. These even included the tricky retail banking undertakings.

Chinese lawyers and legal scholars talk of the need to deepen law reform in China, using terms like 'administrative rule of law'. But the common declaration that 'rule of law' does not mean 'rule by law' underlines a unique feature of what China has done over the last three decades. The whole legal system still comes under the central Ministry of Justice, and the Minister of Justice reports to the national State Council. The head of that is the Chinese Premier, Wen Jiabao. And he also happens to be a major figure on the Standing Committee of the Politburo of the CCP. Just as the army, and the security forces, report finally to the Party, and not to the government, so too do the courts. And any suggestion that they are about to be allowed independence in the near future, sending out judgments against either the government or the Party, is highly optimistic. In China, justice, as well as power, as Mao Zedong once famously said, comes from the barrel of a gun!

The fundamental principles of Chinese legal practice are aligned more with the Continental than with the British system. There is a desire, as one legal scholar said in 2010, to make everything derive from codes. Precedents and case studies, while used, are not liked. Part of this is due to the central importance of the constitution, passed in 1982, and revised four times since. From this document, and its 140 articles, are meant to be derived the powers of specific bodies and entities, of citizens, and of enterprises. The constitution defines rights, responsibilities and parameters of influence and power. Despite early promises, however, it does not define the limits of Party and government. To this day, this elemental divide remains in place, with no clear clarification of duties and responsibilities.

There is widespread recognition that this is becoming an increasing problem, along with an equally widespread belief, at least in the Party, that this is the way things must stay. A former Politburo member in 2007, Luo Gan, in the Party theory magazine *Seeking Truth (Qiu Shi)* stated that lawyers would not be allowed to challenge the legitimacy of the Party and its monopoly on power in China.[25] In 2010, therefore, there is the paradoxical situation of one of the world's key economic powers, with one of the largest economies, and the largest export capacity, and a major external investor, still depriving lawyers active in civil cases of their right to practise law, largely for political rather than legal reasons. Two defenders of Falun Gong cases, for instance, had their licences taken from them for life in May 2010. During their hearings, their attempts to defend themselves were shouted down. The case brought against intellectual and writer Liu Xiaobo for subversion in December 2009, referred to in previous chapters, was held in closed session with his lawyer disallowed from attending before the sentence was handed out. The high-profile Rio Tinto case, where four Shanghai-based employees involved in negotiating prices with Chinese customers were arrested and put on trial in 2009 accused of corruption and insider trading, was made even more controversial by the refusal, against international consular agreements, to allow observers access. Evidence of political interference in courts is plentiful.

The need for a rule-based society, however, is acknowledged by almost everyone, with one of the most prominent leftists, Pan Wei of Beijing University, stating that now that the reform programme in China has led to such economic success, it needs to enter a period of deeper and more far-reaching administrative reform, which will need a far stronger role for the rule of law.[26] On fundamental issues that arouse pubic ire, however, there is little indication that the Party is willing to bite the bullet and allow courts to issue decisions based on clarified laws. Land ownership rights remain undecided, with many petitions to the central government arising from conflicts over title to land and compensation agreements when the land is requisitioned by the state for other purposes. As examples in Chapter 2 showed, local officials continue to supplement their budgets by selling off farmland, much of it against clear central regulations and laws which forbid more development on greenfield sites to protect agricultural land.

Not for the faint of heart: the story of Gao Zhisheng[27]

In his autobiography, Gao Zhisheng, a native of one of the poorest areas of central China, refers to his upbringing in the final years of the Maoist era. 'It is my hope that those who read my essays', he writes, 'and those who know the hardship that surrounds my family and me will not view it as hardship that merely a few individuals are facing. It is actually a window through which one can see the lasting pain of a nation.'[28] The willingness of Gao (himself a Christian) to take on highly contentious legal cases was always a risk. Largely self-taught, he had become one of the first to train as a lawyer in the 1980s, when China had a critical lack of legal personnel. His early cases in the 1990s involved disputes over compensation, and aggrieved businessmen who felt they had been treated unjustly by local officials. But after the clampdown on the Falun Gong sect in 1999 when over 10,000 followers surrounded the central government leadership compound, Zhongnanhai, in Beijing, Gao moved into the far more difficult and sensitive territory of representing cases of those accused of being sect followers and claiming brutal treatment and torture in jail.

Gao had been a Communist Party member for much of his career, and recognised by the Ministry of Justice for his work as recently as 2001–02. But his increasing politicisation as the decade went on, along with his conversion to Christianity, meant than by 2005 he was writing open letters to President Hu demanding a stop to the state-security persecution of Falun Gong followers.

In December 2006, Gao was given a three-year jail sentence for 'inciting subversion'; this was suspended, though he remained under tight surveillance. In 2007, he wrote an eloquent denunciation of the official treatment of some of China's 'bad elements' for the United States Congress. His reward was to be detained by security personnel in September 2007 and placed for weeks in the same kind of hell as lived in by those he had been defending. His account of this experience is searing:

> My pants were falling down around my knees and I was dragged into a room [after they first took me in]. No one had said anything at all to me until that time. The hood was pulled off of my head at this time. Immediately men began cursing and hitting me. '***, your date of death has come today. Brothers, let's give him a brutal lesson today. Beat him to death.'[29]

First beaten with cattle prods, he was then struck repeatedly in the face. Stripped naked, he was held up by his hair and warned, 'Your matter is not only between you and the government.' Promised several courses of treatment, he was repeatedly subjected to electric shocks overnight. The next day, smoke was blown into his face, partially blinding him. Toothpicks were then inserted into his testicles. While he had passed out, some of the tormentors urinated on his face. As his chief interrogator stated, 'This is China. It is the Communist Party's territory. To capture your life is as easy as stepping on an ant. If you dare to continue to write your stupid articles, that government has to make its attitude clear.' Only after signing a confession admitting to womanising and illegal activities was Gao eventually let free.

Some of those who met Gao Zhisheng after his release say that he emerged from this experience half-dead and psychologically damaged. He looked like a broken man. But his ordeal was to deepen. In February 2009 he was abducted in Shanxi province, reportedly while seeking to leave China (he had already helped his wife and daughter to get to Thailand, whence they reached the United States in March 2009). After his disappearance, Gao became a non-person:

no trial was held, no charges were brought, no official statement was made, nothing more was heard of him. Gao Zhisheng vanished. In September 2009, Gao's brother approached the public-security bureau and asked whether there was any news of his whereabouts. He received the baffling reply that Gao had 'gone missing while in detention'; perhaps an indirect admission that in fact he was dead, or in such a poor physical state after yet more ill-treatment that it was no longer possible to show him to the world. In January 2010, a journalist's enquiry for more information solicited another display of masterful ambiguity from a Chinese Foreign Ministry spokesperson, who declared: 'Gao is where he should be.' Reports had him living in Xinjiang, and on retreat at a Buddhist monastery near Mount Wutai.

Gao seems finally to have resurfaced briefly in Beijing in March 2010. He stated in a short meeting with the Associated Press that he had renounced his former life as a lawyer, and that he wanted now to be left alone. Almost as soon as he did this, he disappeared again. Up to the end of November 2010, nothing further has been heard of him. Even hardened human rights defenders dealing with China find Gao's case baffling. 'It is very odd indeed for the authorities simply to say nothing about where someone is. That is like the disappeared in Latin America', said one I spoke to in early 2010. Gao's treatment indicates two facts: that China's security services have become increasingly powerful and assertive in the period since the unrest in Tibet and Xinjiang; and that lawyers who stray into the wrong areas should expect the worst.

Despite this deteriorating environment, however, lawyers have increasingly asserted what rights are granted them, and those they represent, under Chinese law. They have done this at considerable personal cost, and with great integrity. The counsels for the Rio Tinto Four, for instance, were, according to one observer, fiercely assertive in court, and represented their clients with great professionalism and passion. This made it clearer that the outcome was determined more by political rather than by legal factors. As one commentator said: 'If all those involved in the same scams as the people in Rio Tinto in Shanghai were put in court, most of the mining business in China would disappear.'[30] There was little doubt among those who spoke about this case in China in May 2010 that the four were guilty. But nor was there much doubt that had they stuck to the rules, they would have been unable to do their job. They were evidently put in an impossible position.

The Communist Party cannot just walk away from the law, however. Not only is it important for building social stability, but, more crucially, it lies at the heart of the country's future economic development. Take Shanghai. The city's aspirations to be a major international financial centre have been expressed endlessly over the last few years. Dr Fang Xinghai is director general of the city's Financial Services Office. In an interview in April 2010 he stated that 'the State Council directive is mainly to speed up Shanghai's transformation... Shanghai will be among the top three [financial centres] in the world as early as 2015.'[31] But the price of achieving that status – a truly viable independent commercial law system, with all the implications that would carry – is still clearly not one the Communist Party and its key agents are willing to contemplate. There is a sense, therefore, that far from this being their true objective, the real aim is for Shanghai to become a national finance centre, satisfied with servicing one of the fastest developing domestic markets in the world, and to continue relying on Hong Kong and other major centres to do the international finance work. As Fang said in the same interview quoted above, 'We don't want to make an international financial centre for the sake of being an international finance centre. We want it to serve the interests of the people.'

What operatives in the Shanghai system do know is the crucial need for better-educated and trained personnel – but the imperative is to serve social stability through being politically reliable, rather than through creating something that resembles a Western capitalist system. If Shanghai were to want to become a major global centre, the hurdles at the moment would prove insurmountable.

Would global companies, for instance, seriously look to set up headquarters in the city, and locate all of their back-office functions there? Practical questions like this focus the mind on just how far Shanghai has to go. Intellectual property (IP) issues are another key area. Shanghai sees itself as an area where other places in China can come to innovate. But that sort of space, while interesting to domestic innovators, carries little attraction for those outside China. The issues of government control and interference in the economy are hard to ignore. Former Party secretary of the city, Chen Liangyu, before he was felled for corruption in 2006, famously boasted that Shanghai's economy was 80 per cent state directed. Its brash entrepreneurial exterior is just that – a veneer.[32] At its heart lurks the same all-pervasive party-state, as elsewhere in the country. The CCP is willing to admit that it needs help in improving its administrative capacity. So while the opportunities for outsiders to lecture China on the faults of its own system are drying up (there are plenty of excellent Chinese experts who are all too aware of where their system needs improvement) and there is even less appetite than in the past for thinking about fully independent courts, there is greater space for technical cooperation. The training of judges, for instance, remains critical, with whole areas of legal practice being new, or relatively new, and needing well-trained adjudicators.

In the last decade, the Party has talked more about having its own law, and disciplining itself. In the early part of 2007, the feared Central Discipline and Inspection Commission (CDIC) descended on Shanghai, where powerful Party secretary Chen Liangyu, referred to above, a member of the Politburo, had been placed under house arrest. Three hundred investigators trawled through the books of the city, tracing back massive payments that had gone into various funds, trying to link them to an enormous property scam. Only a couple of years later, a similar group went into Chongqing, to clean up the mafia links there, under the high-profile Party secretary Bo Xilai. The CDIC is a law unto itself, but, as one legal expert in

China stated in the summer of 2009, 'The Party, and only the Party, disciplines itself. The organisation department in the Party centrally in Beijing alone can take a Party secretary in a province to task. In their own locality, they are simply above the law.' No court would be crazy enough, in this vertical system, to challenge the powers of the Party. China awaits its 1803 moment, when, in the case of *Marbury* v. *Madison*, the US Supreme Court decided that it could overturn a law passed by Congress if it contravened the Constitution. 'The Party knows that the future will see growth slow down', another expert in Beijing said. 'It sees its legitimacy being based on performance, and recently it has tried to identify more closely those key constituents or groups in society that it must maintain the support of. Rural groups are one of these. Its other great objective is to create internal accountability measures.' This lies behind the efforts to shift away from the experiment with Party elections, and more to delivering democracy in the Party. This is dealt with below.

The possibility of real crisis within the system, causing either limited or total collapse of governance, cannot be overestimated, and that fact will force change in ways which are entirely unforeseen at present. In Chinese politics, history has taught us to expect the unexpected. It is amazing how often that lesson is forgotten. In many practical ways the court system is already broken. It is unable to deal with the number of cases put before it. According to government data, in 1978, across the country, there were 447,000 trial cases. In 2008, this had risen to 6.2 million. In 1978 cases split almost one-third to two-thirds criminal to civil. Thirty years later, while criminal cases had gone up to 767,000, the number of civil cases had rocketed to 5.4 million.[33] Those who fail to find satisfaction in the courts are left with the sole route of making a petition to the central government (see the next section). The inability of courts to deal with the number of disputes is a huge institutional challenge. In China, in 2010, courts are under siege, with failings in their impartiality, their ability to deliver justice, and their personnel – and that, for a CCP trying to create a more just society, is a big problem.

What happens to those who dare to petition

The petition (*xinfan*) system as it currently exists in the PRC harks back to imperial times, when people dissatisfied with the response of local officials to grievances were able to pursue their case in higher levels of government, gradually working up to the central administration. In the twenty-first century this system has returned. Lengthy depositions are made first at provincial level, then to central government, usually ending up in Beijing at the State Bureau for Letters and Visits.[34]

Petitions have increased in number in the last decade, and particularly since 2003. Over 10 million were dealt with centrally over that period.[35] Since 2008 they have shot up even more steeply. Julie Harms, a Harvard graduate and US citizen, became perhaps the first foreigner to try to make a petition through the system, after her Chinese boyfriend was put on trial for trespass. In 2009 she attempted to deliver a petition to the prosecutor's office in Beijing. No one was there to take it, and her only success was getting a shouted call from a man inside, through an iron grill covering the door, for her to go away as the office was closed. Further attempts to deliver her petition in the right way were also rebuffed.[36] She was spared the fate of many others. A combination of nervousness around the Olympics about the number of outsiders coming up to lodge complaints, and new measures brought in to hold local officials accountable for the number of complaints coming from their districts, have meant that active measures are now being taken to stop petitioners.

Human Rights Watch issued a report based on the testimony of about fifty of those who had been through the system. Retrievers – basically thugs employed by private security companies to work on contracts granted by local authorities – are sent to Beijing to round up petitioners, and deal with them. This means time in a network of 'black jails', wholly outside the criminal system, run for profit, and containing as many as 10,000 inmates at any one time. Black jails can exist in hostels or hotels, or even beside the very offices for the provinces the petitions might relate to. In this grim underground, people simply disappear. They are subjected to sexual and physical abuse, denied access to medical treatment, subjected to food and sleep deprivation, and threatened. People sometimes disappear into the system for months, even years. Often only payment of extortionate fees and signing papers relinquishing their case allows them freedom. Black jails literally remove people from the whole system, submerging them for a period before releasing them, frightened, back into their communities, where they are able to spread the word that making a petition carries terrifying consequences. Those who most persistently make petitions are often regarded as having mental-health problems. Some even end up in psychiatric prisons. In view of the trauma they go through, this is hardly surprising, and could almost be named a syndrome in its own right – 'petition condition'.

Civil society

Several times over the last few years, the annual Chinese parliament, the NPC, has debated the role of civil society and NGOs, and what sort of status to give them. This has been a constant problem. Since the 1980s, the Chinese state has redrawn its areas of activity. There are many services and issues it no longer wishes to get involved with. Drawing on a history of civil society groups reaching back to the Republican Era and the Qing Dynasty, a raft of organisations have grown up dealing with issues from the care of children and the elderly, to faith-based groups, to charities. One of the most vibrant areas has been in environmental activism (see the next section). The state has tolerated, and even encouraged, these groups, with the Ministry of Civil Affairs in Beijing estimating that there may be as many as 240,000, spread across the country. But, wary of the role that non-governmental groups played in the Colour Revolutions across Europe and Central Asia after the fall of the USSR, a controlling framework has been set up. In the late 1980s, three laws were passed, just before the Tiananmen Square event in June 1989, which created a two-tier system of management for civil society groups. All groups had to register with the Ministry of Civil Affairs. They also had to have their finances scrutinised by the government through this agency. Around the irritation caused by the Falun Gong movement in the late 1990s, the NPC passed new laws, one of which, the Public Welfare Donations Law, granted vague tax exemption for NGOs under certain circumstances, while leaving the need to register with the government in place.[37]

In the last decade, things have grown more complicated. Government-organised non-governmental organisations (GONGOs) have continued to exist – organisations like the sanctioned trade union, the All China Federation of Trade and Industry for businesses and entrepreneurs, and the All China Women's Federation. But they have become increasingly dependent on membership rather than government funding. In addition to them, a whole raft of international NGOs have also started working in China, ranging from groups like Save the Children Fund, which has run projects in Tibet and the Western region of China, to Oxfam. Many civil society groups have also tried to get around the confusing tax payment rules by simply registering with the Ministry of Commerce, and having that as their sponsoring department.

Society has also continued to become more complex. AIDS groups and organisations promoting equal rights for gays have come into existence, bringing issues that were largely taboo right up to the 1990s into the mainstream. Others have worked with migrant children, dealing with the educational needs of a group which is largely discriminated against and marginalised. Again, this has been deemed legitimate work by local and national government and been allowed to continue unimpeded. Consumer protection groups, and legal aid providers, have also sprung up. Many groups (of which Open Constitution Initiative was one, before it was closed down) were linked to university departments, from which they derived their patronage and their legal, and sometimes political, protection.

Hu Jia's story is the kind that most worries the authorities. Born in 1973, just as the Cultural Revolution was coming to an end, Hu was a high-school student during the disturbances in 1989. After university in the 1990s, he became involved in the emerging environmentalist

Environmental NGOs

In light of mounting environmental problems, it is not surprising that this has been an area where civil society has become most active. According to the American specialist on the Chinese environment, Elizabeth Economy, a whole raft of such groups were set up from the 1990s onwards as the impact of China's rapid industrialisation on nature started to become clear, and elements of the Green agenda developed in the West began to register in China. One of the best known of these, Friends of Nature, was founded by Liang Congjie, grandson of Liang Qichao, one of the most prominent reformers in early-twentieth-century China (see Chapter 1). Another, a campaign to save the Yunnan snub-nosed monkey and Tibetan antelope, received national coverage in the 1990s, despite the two main activists being forbidden from registering as an NGO by the local government. Green Volunteer League and Green River have been successful regional pressure groups.[38]

That NGOs can creep into sensitive areas very easily, even in a space where environmental concerns are often articulated as much by the government as by any other group in society, is something Economy acknowledges. Indeed, activists have tended to transfer their activities in order to avoid trouble. But as the celebrated case of the polluted Lake Taihu shows, even those who establish NGOs on issues that the central government has expressed a positive view are still vulnerable. Lake Taihu, between the highly industrialised Zhejiang and Jiangsu provinces, was contaminated by many factories discharging polluted water into it in the 2000s, leading to massive surface algae problems. In 2007, a local activist Wu Lihong, who had raised the issue of the Lake right up to the level of the NPC, was sentenced to three years in jail for extortion, though it was clear to many observers at the time that his real crime was to have irritated local officials with his persistent campaign. Released in May 2010, Wu claimed that he had been badly beaten while in prison: 'It's obvious that the authorities have sought to harm me', he told journalists by phone after his release. 'I will continue to appeal the conviction and seek to clear my name.'[39]

movement and linked up with the Friends of Nature. He was also involved in the Tibetan antelope preservation group. But this was only a step towards AIDS activism work in the early 2000s, and increasing radicalism. Hu migrated towards the arena of citizen activism, protesting during the highly sensitive 4 June anniversary period in Beijing in the mid-2000s, and being detained first in 2006, and then in 2007. His final trial in 2008 resulted in a three-and-a-half-year prison sentence. Reports in April 2010 suggest that he might have liver cancer. Hu Jia's case sits alongside that of Chen Guangcheng, of Shandong province, who angered the authorities in 2005 by reporting on forced abortions in the district in which he lived. Chen, who is blind, was imprisoned for four and a half years in 2006. Released in September 2010, he was placed under house detention immediately afterwards, severely limiting his contact with the outside world. As one long-term observer of the treatment of dissidents in contemporary China commented, 'One gets the impression that the government just wants these people to rot away and die quietly.' Citizen activism linked to any NGO has been a high-risk route for these people.

The position in which NGOs find themselves in China is not helped by their highly precarious legal and financial existence. 'They are worse to deal with than the government', one executive dealing with Chinese NGOs in a multinational company based in China complained in 2008. 'They fight against each other, trying to carve out some territory for themselves. At least the government is more unified than that.' This is, in view of the situation, not that surprising. A Chinese NGO has to live with the threat of potential harassment from the government, the need to stay close to a source of patronage, and finally the sheer lack of capacity and money. 'NGOs', said someone in 2009 who had set up a group to help them, 'don't know how to get funding. They don't know how to manage themselves. They have no experience of building up capacity. And the moment that they become prominent, the government starts to take a close interest in them.' Even highly experienced international NGOs are not immune from falling into traps. Nick Young, who ran

China Development Brief for a number of years highly successfully in Beijing, had his whole operation curtailed, and his right to work in China, and even to visit, withdrawn in 2007. He was never given a clear reason why someone who had largely concentrated on the gathering of neutral information on development societies in China was receiving such curt, rough treatment from the government.

In 2010 the situation continued to deteriorate. An NGO focusing on women's rights, linked to Beijing University, the Center for Women's Law Studies and Legal Services, received a cancellation notice on 25 March. This effectively meant that the Center either found another patron or ceased to exist legally. One of its founders, Guo Jianmei, stated on 2 April that the cancellation was 'a major and unexpected change for an organization that has been striving and fighting continuously for 15 years.'[40] In 2009 one of the main AIDS activists, Dr Gao Yaojie, decided to stay on in the USA after a visit because she said she feared returning to China. In early May 2010 Wan Yanhai, another of the country's prominent activists, who had established a highly respected NGO in Beijing called Aizhixing ('Love, knowledge, action') also moved to the USA with his family, saying that he had no other choice because 'the attacks from the government had become very serious for my organization and for me personally. I had concerns about my personal safety and was under a lot of stress.'[41] Since his departure, the offices of Aizhixing in Beijing have been raided, with demands, as in the case of Open Constitution a year before, for a full account of foreign funding, and the back-payment of monies regarded now as taxable which had originally been accepted as non-taxable.

The CCP clearly has a highly ambiguous relationship with NGOs. While willing to tolerate large swathes of civil society, it grows increasingly nervous when anything remotely like a political agenda appears. And yet, in the rural areas in which elections occur, NGOs do important work, on the environment, education and health care. What is the Party's and government's problem with this? Why do they continue to do so little about the legal status of NGOs, and

Why the CCP wants to avoid becoming a second USSR

In the West, a good deal of commentary about the fall of the Soviet Union is triumphalist, viewing it as an untrammelled good. One very senior member of the first George W. Bush presidency, when the mention of Gorbachev came up over a dinner I attended in Britain in 2006, immediately raised his glass and proposed a toast to 'a man who did the right thing'. For China, though, at both elite and popular levels, what happened in Russian society when the Soviet Union collapsed is a blueprint for everything it wishes to avoid. The economic collapse of the country in the 1990s, its loss of international prestige, the falling away of parts of the USSR into independence, the massive health problems suffered, which saw average male mortality rates soar for five years, are only the worst side effects of the change. Even under the Putin presidency, which at least saw Russia rebuild itself, it is still regarded as a country that botched things. Many in Russia look at China's huge growth rates enviously, and wonder whether Gorbachev wasn't wrong, in the end, to act as he did.

Early assessments from within China just as the collapse happened had to deal with the crisis of faith which the whole series of events brought for Chinese communists. Chinese Sovietologist Pan Deli wrote in 1990 that the key mistake of the Gorbachev leadership was to give political reform priority over economic reform, allow the growth of an opposition, tolerate ethnic divisions in the Union, and rely too much on the West. In 1996, further analysis commissioned by the government under Jiang Zemin argued that Gorbachev's adoption of humanism and democratic socialism was the key problem, recommending that the CCP had to insist on 'Party unity, manage internal struggle better, improve cadre selection, strengthen the grassroots organisations, and fight against corruption'.[42] The Soviet Union's management of the economy and abandonment of key ideological territory were singled out for particular blame. In surveys in Beijing carried out by academic Neil Munro in 2007, canvassing views on the reasons behind the Soviet collapse, policymakers and scholars cited as the key ones excess centralisation of power, ideological rigidity, lack of Party democracy and economic problems. They made clear that the CCP needed to learn from the fate of the Soviet Union by placing itself at the centre of social and national unity, and preserving stability.[43] The one thing these experts didn't say was that the Soviet Union's fate offered anything positive for the CCP to copy.

place such enormous pressure on some kinds of NGOs? There is a simple answer to this, and that is the possible link between groups like these and an issue the CCP finds the most sensitive and difficult of all – the possibility, one day, of organised political opposition.

Organised political opposition: the final frontier

Organised political opposition is the great elephant in the room in all talk of rural democracy and elections. In the summer of 2009, as I talked to people about village elections, and tried to understand better the technical aspects of the law, organisation and management of elections, there was one question which kept nagging at me, but which I didn't openly discuss. What happens if there is some traction between independents who stand in elections in Chinese villages? Non-Party members, for instance, who put themselves up, and then win seats, and find that they have a common cause with other non-party members – at what point does this common cause between them become a nascent organised political opposition? Would a group of two or three non-Party Village Committee leaders meeting together to discuss issues be the moment the line had been crossed? Would an informal support network for non-Party leaders be the tipping point? Would it be the fearful moment when a small number openly say that they do, in fact, have a common programme – greater land rights, for instance, or anti-corruption – and that the solution for this is discussion about the monopoly on power of the CCP?

The CCP has not tolerated any form of organised political opposition at all. The last attempt was in 1998, during the era of Jiang Zemin, when a group largely based in the city of Hangzhou, in

Zhejiang province, tried to register an independent political party. During a visit by then US president Bill Clinton, Wang Youcai, an activist veteran of the June 4th Movement in 1989 then living in Hangzhou, went to the local government office to register the China Democracy Party (CDP). Its membership was a handful of fellow 1989ers. That was in June. Only a month later, he was formally detained and indicted. A few months later, at the end of the year, Xu Wenli, whose career as a veteran activist went back to the Democracy Wall movement at the end of the 1970s, announced the establishment of a Beijing–Tianjin branch of the CDP. Unlike Wang Youcai, they did not attempt to register it, saying that there were no laws in the PRC covering the operation of political parties, and therefore they were free to create one. Yu Tieling, a CDP member, ran the same month in a village election in Zhejiang province as an independent, only to have his candidacy nullified by the local township officials. A meeting of CDP activists in Hangzhou on 20 November was broken up by police, with Wu Yiling, the owner of the house in which the meeting was taking place, detained and two others sent back to their residences in Shanghai, two hours away. Several other people at this meeting were also subsequently arrested. The same day, Xie Wanjun, who had threatened to hold a demonstration in Tiananmen Square as a protest at the crackdown on the party, was detained, his wife was sacked from her job, and the electricity to his house was cut off.

To symbolise the Party's views on this grassroots mini-rebellion, Premier Li Peng, reviled because he had been closely associated with the implementation of a crackdown on student demonstrations on 4 June 1989, gave an interview to a journalist from the German *Der Spiegel* newspaper on 23 November, stating that the CDP activists were trying to return the country to the chaos of the Cultural Revolution. He castigated the 'boisterous chaos' of Western parliaments, stating that 'If an organization lobbies for the multiparty system, trying to oppose the leadership of the Communist Party, then it will not be allowed to exist.'

Wang Youcai was formally charged on 30 November with 'subverting state power', conspiring with foreign forces by fax and email, and accepting foreign funding. Xu Wenli was finally detained the same day, his house searched, and his computer and paperwork confiscated. Qin Yongmin was also indicted for 'subversion', for his role in partnering Xu in establishing the CDP Beijing Tianjin branch. Xu Wanping was sentenced to three years 'reform through labour' in early December for his links to the CDP, at the same time as several activists in Liaoning province, who had put together a petition protesting the CDP clampdown, were detained. On 4 December, Ren Wanding, another Democracy Wall veteran and associate of Xu Wenli, was detained in Beijing and told to stop all CDP-related work. Four days later, on 8 December, Zhang Baoqin in Fujian and Liu Xianbin in Sichuan were detained on charges of being CDP supporters. Yao Zhenxian, a Shanghai businessman who supported the CDP, after being charged with what were largely regarded as fabricated charges for possessing pornography, fled China on 9 December. On 10 December, Wang Ce, long-time resident in Spain after leaving China in the 1980s, and chair of the overseas Chinese Democracy Party, was arrested while trying to present a letter to the Chinese Consultative Political People's Congress about the anti-CDP purge after having re-entered the country. Caught while in Hangzhou, he was accused of 'sponsoring activities that endangered the state's safety' and 'furtively crossing the border'. As he was being held in Hangzhou, two CDP sympathisers in Sichuan were picked up for trying to mount a protest in support of Wang Youcai the same day. The lawyer preparing to defend Wang, Wang Wenjiang (no relation), was arrested by police while trying to board the train from his home in Liaoning to Hangzhou. The vice chair of the CDP's Hubei branch, Qin Yongmin, was detained on 12 December. On 14 December, 184 activists sent an open letter to then president Jiang Zemin demanding a fair trial for Wang. Over the 15th and 16th, eleven of these were detained in Hangzhou after they attempted to attend Wang's trial and mount a vigil outside the courthouse. In a speech celebrating the twentieth anniversary of the Reform and Opening Up period, President Jiang simply remarked, on 18 December, that, 'From beginning to end, we must be vigilant against infiltration, subversive activities, and separatist activities of international and domestic hostile forces.'

Over the two days from 21 to 22 December, Xu Wenli, Wang Youcai and Qin Yongmin were sentenced. In Beijing, Xu received thirteen years in prison for organising the CDP, promoting independent trade unions and giving interviews to foreign journalists (he had, for instance, been interviewed by the BBC during the visit by the new prime minister of the UK, Tony Blair, to China in late 1998). Wang Youcai was sentenced to eleven years, in Hangzhou, with his lawyer finally able to defend him at the trial, despite having himself been detained four times over the four days he had tried to get to Hangzhou. In his summary statement to the judge, he had been unable to speak. No foreign observers were allowed into the courtroom. Qin Yongmin was sentenced to twelve years, and did not even have a trial lawyer to defend him.[44]

That ended the brief flowering of the China Democracy Party movement. Wang Youcai was exiled from China to the USA in 2004, and now serves as co-chairman of the CDP in New York. Xu Wenli was exiled to the USA on medical grounds in 2002, and now works as an academic at Brown University, Providence, Rhode Island. Qin Yongmin remained in jail as of 2009, despite appeals by his wife on grounds of his ill health.

The fate of those who supported the CDP during its brief life makes one thing absolutely clear: that to set up organised political opposition to the CCP is for the very brave or the very foolish. The authorities are willing to commit formidable resources and time to stamping out every last vestige of any entities that dare to oppose them. And, so far, this tactic has worked well. There is not even the weakest political entity in the PRC that can challenge the CCP. Brutal repression and responses have worked. In this last great area of taboo activity, to this day those who stray within can expect their lives to be invaded by security agents, and to spend long years in prison.

Yet there is a question mark over just how sustainable this response is. One day, maybe many years from now, or maybe far sooner than we might expect, the CCP will need to deal with political opposition more creatively. It might have to engage with forces that it regards as threats, but without being able to lock up their operatives or frighten them into silence. There is no sense, now Taiwan has become a vibrant democracy, in saying that somehow multiparty structures are not compatible with Chinese culture. One day, just as in Taiwan, repression will not work. And the question will be then, how will the CCP engage with something that, until now, it hasn't even let out into the light of day? For the moment, the CCP thinks it has the answer: intra-Party democracy – that is to say, democracy within the Party, on its own terms, in its own way.

Keeping its own house in order: democracy within the CCP

At the NPC annual meeting in March 2010, Premier Wen Jiabao admitted in his government work report that 'the state's hold on power could be threatened by the combined effects of inflation, social injustice and official corruption.' The Chinese state now spends almost as much money on internal security (US\$75 billion) as it does on external security (US\$80 billion).[45] Corruption is the malignant cancer on the Chinese body politic, and eats away at the legitimacy of the CCP. But the CCP is the sole entity that is able to regulate itself. This paradox throws up increasing problems as the nation modernises, grows wealthy and becomes more entrepreneurial. The pact that the CCP has forged with other social forces, from business people to NGOs and intellectuals, dilutes its own holy mission from the 1940s to represent the workers and productive forces in society, slowly moving towards a socialist Utopia in the years ahead.

Those that look for the evidence for corruption need, more often than not, only rest their eyes on the nearest middle- to senior-level

Party official in their midst. *Financial Times* journalist Richard Mc-Gregor summarises just a few cases from a short period in 2009:

> the railway bureau chief in Urumqi, in far-west Xinjiang, was charged with embezzling US$3.6 million; in Shanghai, a mid-level official in charge of property was convicted of taking US$1 million in bribes and forced to divest himself of real estate worth nearly US$6 million; in a small rural township near Chengdu, in Sichuan, the Party Secretary and head of the local, real estate company was executed for taking US$2.5 million in bribes; in the poorest town in Guangdong, the local police chief was discovered with US$4.4 million in cash at home; in Chongqing, western China, the head of a development zone went on trial for misappropriating US$32.1 million and taking bribes of US$1.4 million in a case involving thirty other officials; in Changchun, in the north-east rustbelt, the police chief of a single district was found with US$1.9 million in cash in his office; and in Suzhou, the vice-mayor in charge of construction was sentenced for taking about US$12 million, the largest one-off bribe on record.[46]

Money washes in and out of Party officials' coffers. In public surveys, such corruption recurs time and time again as a source of anger and discontent for urban and rural residents. The Party's attempts to regulate itself through the Central Inspectorate and Discipline Commission are ad hoc, and always need the highest level political support. But when every member of the Standing Committee of the Politburo has also been linked with corruption, this undermines confidence that the Party can ever truly control its own affairs and get its house in order.

Since the mid-2000s, Hu Jintao, as part of the process of putting his own mark on society, started to authorise more talk of democracy, not at the grassroots, or in townships, but within the Party itself. The logic for this was simple. As noted above, the CCP has often looked like a state within a state, with its own internal dynamics, institutions and political programme. One theory in the last few years has been that to achieve the dual objectives of ensuring its own long-term power in China, and of introducing ideas about democratic accountability with greater control to wider society, intra-Party democracy – democracy within the CCP first of all – was a good solution.

There is no elite consensus on this, and a good amount of argument about exactly what such a concept actually means. Putting democracy on hold elsewhere while the CCP embeds it in its own operations seems counter-intuitive. Surely the whole point of democracy would be to challenge the CCP's monolithic hold on power in key areas. But supporters at the top level in the CCP, including Wen Jiabao and the head of the Organisation Department (in effect, the CCP's personnel department) and member of the full Politburo Li Yuanchao, have made it clear that without addressing its own governance, and starting to become more transparent and accountable, the CCP is going to have a very difficult future. As Cheng Li, long-term observer of elite politics in China has observed, at a September 2009 meeting in Beijing, leaders agreed that 'careful management of the Party has never been so arduous and urgent… intra-Party democracy is the lifeblood of the Party.'[47] While Party secretary of the dynamic coastal province of Jiangsu from 2001 to 2007, before his elevation to Beijing, Li Yuanchao, a former student at the Kennedy School of Governance at Harvard, and a princeling (related to a former senior leader in the Party), adopted elections within the local Party for key positions. In this, he has been followed by another likely rising star for the post-2012 leadership, Wang Yang of Guangdong, who has allowed discussion of elections for mayor and vice mayor of Shenzhen since his arrival as Party boss of the important province in 2007.

This more liberal wing is ranged against hardliners – of whom the two most prominent current spokespeople are Wu Bangguo, number two in the Standing Committee, and Jia Qinglin, number four, and a protégé of former president Jiang Zemin, and a man deeply mired in the corruption scandals involving billions of yuan in Fujian province in the late 1990s. Jia's standing as the most corrupt and unpopular politician in the current line-up puts him in the same distinguished company as Li Peng and other historic hardliners in the past. His lambasting of Western-style democracy, as opposed to 'the Chinese way', has frequently been publicly unleashed on the body that he presides over, the CCPPC. For Wu Bangguo, a man of deep mystery, who in the last two decades has risen from nowhere to become the second most powerful man in the country, with seemingly no factional or elite patronage to support his elevation (something against all the laws of contemporary Chinese politics), his heading of the NPC is again of no weight when fuming against 'multiparty systems' from the West which would bring instability into China. Wu is famous for issuing sharp instructions before major meetings to Party members telling them to toe the line, even about issues that have already long been openly discussed. That the Politburo contains such a rich array of heroes and villains is good for the narrative of modern Chinese politics, and helps to keep vast armies of Hong Kong and foreign journalists gainfully employed in rich speculative adventures (Jia, famously, was already dead man walking before 2007, when he was, many said, sure to be removed from his slot. To general embarrassment, he walked out in the higher number four position, defying predictions – and natural justice, perhaps). But it creates havoc with the key issue of Wu's capacity to instil Party discipline, which intra-Party democracy was meant to cure.

Expert on the contemporary CCP Cheng Li comes up with five key objectives that the CCP hopes to achieve through intra-Party democracy. The first is to make positions open to genuine competition, along the same lines as the multi-candidate elections in villages. Since 1982, as he points out, the principle of having more candidates than positions has been accepted, at least within the elite Central Committee. In 2007, for instance, for the 204 Central Committee full slots (and this is the elite of Party leadership, including heads of huge SOEs, leaders of provinces, directors of key universities, etc.) there were 221 candidates. Such elections can be meaningful. In the past, princelings have fared badly, with people like Bo Xilai, currently Politburo member and Party secretary of Chongqing, failing to receive popular support in the late 1990s to enter the Central Committee. Famously, the current number six in the whole system and likely replacement for Hu Jintao as Party secretary and country president in 2012, Xi Jinping, only just scraped into the Central Committee in 1997, with the smallest number of votes. The central issue, however, of having any wide voting for membership of the Politburo, either the Standing Committee or the full one, is currently unthinkable. Key slots remain very much in the hands of a tight, and very opaque, core of senior leaders.

The second issue is for voting within the Party to show consensus in policymaking, and for there to be votes for policies, involving large infrastructure projects, social policy, security issues, and so on. And again, while more issues have been put to the Party membership in various forms, key matters are still very much kept in the hands of the Party elite. As part of a process of building greater institutionalisation and also having rules by which it can regulate its own affairs, for the third issue, there have been more controls on leaders. Senior leaders have to retire, usually by the age of 67. They can only serve two terms in any one position (the Party secretary of Xinjiang, Wang Lequan, was the great exception, having served almost three terms when he stepped down in 2010 – but because of the unique security issues of this region, his case only proved the rule). Finally, Party bosses of provinces are almost never natives of those areas, because of the problems of tribalism and vested interest that this causes. Fourth, there have been more attempts to introduce multidimensional supervision of leaders, through congresses, Party committees and external Party bodies. Finally, moves have been made to make the whole process transparent.

Touming, transparency, has been a key term in the debates about governance over the last few years. Attempts have been made to introduce more open governance, with budgets issued online, and information more widely available via the Internet. Leaders have tried, at most levels, to reach out to people. But there is plenty of evidence that *touming* can only go so far. The example of Bo

Xilai and his well-publicised purge of the mafia in Chongqing over 2009 and into 2010 is a case in point. Speculation still rages about who authorised him to do this, how, and at what level. Rumours swirled around the case, just as they did when Wen Jiabao issued his celebrated recollections of Hu Yaobang, the former reformist leader from the 1980s, in the *People's Daily* in the spring of 2010. Was this a sign of an imminent rehabilitation of the 1989 activists, and a redefinition of the 1989 event as not 'counter-revolutionary', as it had been labelled since then, but a misguided student movement, led by patriotic but muddled students? Or was it a sign of Wen suddenly laying down a reformist gauntlet to his hardline opponents in the elite? In the end, we simply don't know. At the very top, and in its deep hidden corners, the CCP remains as opaque as it ever was. Intra-Party democracy sometimes feels like a superficial change. It does not, and is not meant to, reach the heart of the organisation supporting it.

The CCP's ability to regulate its own affairs and governance will be put to the test in the lead-up to the Eighteenth Party Congress, scheduled for late 2012. This is a big moment for the PRC, and for the Party, simply because never before has there been such a large turnover in positions at the top without there being at least some Party old guard from the original revolutionary movement in the early years to at least steer the process through peacefully. Jiang Zemin's great contribution to history was to step aside in 2002 at the Sixteenth Party Congress, creating the precedent of a supreme leader disappearing. And, despite rumours of his activities behind the scenes, on the whole his influence has gradually diminished, while Hu Jintao's has been able to increase. When his tenure ends in 2012, the CCP will need all the rules, regulations and precedents it has to handle the elevation of probably seven new faces into the nine- strong Standing Committee. With no public votes for this process, nor votes even within the CCP, how will it be achieved? Who will decide which figure gets which slot? What happens in the case of outright conflict between two figures or interest groups?

And when the decision is made, how will it be greeted in the wider society? None of these new figures has anything like the credibility even of recent former leaders. Their political capital grows weaker and weaker. They are purely products brought up within the CCP. They owe everything to it. How can they claim legitimacy when their selection process has been so opaque? These are quandaries that the CCP has been thinking about for a number of years, but will find particularly urgent and pressing in 2012.

Back to the Party School

In Chapter 2 I referred to a blueprint for political reform which had been drawn up in 2007 by key members of the Central Party School in Beijing. Perhaps it is time now to return to this important document and to consider what it states are the key areas needing reform as China develops into the twenty-first century. One of the striking features of the book *Storming the Fortress* is the strategy of the editors and authors to stick carefully to the parameters of Hu Jintao's speech at the Seventeenth Party Congress. In some senses, therefore, the book offers a parallel text to Hu's words, fleshing out some of the details that he gives, and filling in the admittedly very large gaps in what he says about political reform. Hu has been associated closely with the theory of 'putting people first' (*you ren wei ben*). Beyond the stipulation that China's economic reform should continue and deepen, Hu mentions several specific administrative and political areas that are in need of further improvement and development. These are:

1. Participation of people in political affairs.
2. Deepening the rule of law.
3. Deepening fiscal, taxation and financial reform, and the accountability of government for the money that it spends.
4. Promoting social equity and justice.
5. Improving social management.

6. Expanding intra-Party democracy.
7. Improving the education of cadres.

The book's authors state in the Introduction to their work that 'After the Seventeenth Party Congress what we must ask is why does the political system of China need to change, what needs to be changed, how can it be changed, and what is the process of that change.'[48] In their summary they state that the overall aim is to push forward intra-Party democracy through reform of the people's congresses, the government system and the legal system, and 'to create a just [*gongzheng*] and righteous [*zhengyi*] society'. Quoting Hu Jintao, they say that 'with no democracy there is no socialism'.[49] Faced with the continuing problems of sustainable economic development, agricultural and rural reform, social security and stability, and the challenges of the environment, China 'needs a strong [*qiangli*] political system. Without this, we cannot resolve these problems.'[50]

Staying within the broad parameters set by Hu, *Storming the Fortress* divides its blueprint for China's political reform into four broad areas: the rule of law; the training and education of cadres; the management of news and information; and intra-Party democracy.

All of these have been looked at above. But at the very beginning, and indeed throughout their various discussions, the authors clarify one critical piece of ideological certainty: 'Without the leadership of the CPC, there will be no progress in the reform of China's political system, and the development of China as a nation has no future.' Democratic accountability exists, and will be strengthened, by the people's congresses at their various local, provincial and national levels. But while 'in terms of law the congresses are the highest state organs ... in the political life of China, they come under the leadership of the Party.'[51] A similar observation is made about the courts, and about civil society groups, all of which have their crucial functions recognised, but all of which have to come under the political direction of the CCP.

The blueprint of *Storming the Fortress*: the six pillars

The blueprint focuses on six pillars: the proposed reform of congresses; national and local level relations; consultative bodies and their role; the legal system; administrative change; and the fabric of society (i.e. civil society groups and religious issues).

CONGRESSES

The people's congressional system from local to national level is seen as delivering some of the public participation in decision-making that Hu Jintao said was a crucial element of China's political reform (consultative conferences, another means to deliver participation, are discussed below). Congresses 'increase the role of participation'.[52] One of their greatest areas of potential power is in the scrutinizing and approval of budgets. As American political scientist Lynn T. White states, China 'still lacks elections to offices that allocate any substantial resources'.[53] Representatives at congresses, despite being appointed and not elected above township level, are at least able to involve representatives of different areas of society from inside and outside the CCP to look over local and national planned expenditure and to give some degree of feedback, displaying transparency and accountability.

In the view of the authors of *Storming the Fortress*, the current congress system, while in theory offering some control and scrutiny over financial disbursements by various levels of government, in practice suffers from many shortcomings. They list these as: (1) a lack of time and specialist training to scrutinize complex budgets; (2) a need now, after twenty years of elections to Village Committees, to have a wider choice of candidates and more diverse representation on people's congresses, from the township level up, to expand their expertise and give them greater public credibility; (3) a need to scale down the numbers of representatives to make them more manageable. The final point is key. The NPC, with over 3,000 members, is far larger, for instance, than representative assemblies in countries like the USA, India and Russia. For instance, the authors calculate that a single US senator represents some 3 million people; were it the case that each member of the NPC represented a similar number of citizens, the Congress would be reduced to around 400 people. As it stands, the sheer number of those attending makes the NPC unwieldy and unfit for purpose, so that, even with the best will in the world, discussions of issues among so many people is impractical and reverts to formula and stage management. In addition to this, the congresses need to have real powers, and the strongest of these would be to set taxes, for local and central government. The public is either ignorant of the role of the people's congresses, or cynical about them, and having a key function like this would offer them an easily understandable role in the political life of the PRC. Lacking genuine responsibility, they run the risk of being labelled a rubber-stamp entity. A Chinese journalist indeed called the NPC such a thing in 1994, and was rewarded with six years in jail.[54] To be effective, people's congresses need to be genuinely independent, and able to discuss budgets openly. One administrative means of facilitating the achievement of this would be to ensure that the Chinese financial year (which currently runs from January to December) and the convening of the NPC (which is held between March and May) were brought into synchronisation. Congresses should meet nationally in the latter part of the year, around November or December, in order to give feedback on budgets and allow for their proposals to be taken into account, and, where accepted, implemented for January. As things stand, even if the congresses are able to suggest a change, the financial year is already well advanced, watering down the impact of anything they say.

NATIONAL AND LOCAL GOVERNMENT DYNAMICS

China, the authors admit, has 'a history of centralisation of power'. Lack of clarity over where local and national powers lie has created constant tension. This existed before the creation of the PRC, and has resurfaced in various forms since 1949. Defining legitimate areas of local government power is a key responsibility of national government. This is related to the powers divested to the people's congress system (discussed above) and the clear devolution of these through local people's congresses. Local congresses need to be given powers similar to the National Congress, the strongest of which is the ability to sanction the raising of taxes by local governments.

Matters of national importance should remain the responsibility of the central government – for example, aspects of national economic policy, security, energy issues.

Local governments and congresses have a number of major tasks. These divide into allocating resources; enfranchising the floating populations that are either going or returning to an area; representing sparsely populated areas equitably at a national level when fund disbursements occur; and ensuring that natural resources which come from particular areas and raise revenue are then allocated according to where the need is, but also with fairness to the region where the resources came from (this has been a particular issue in areas like Xinjiang, which reportedly has received only a 1 per cent return on minerals and energy resources taken from it). Giving local government an explicit constitutional role is one of the remedies that *Storming the Fortress* proposes, along with suggesting a clear rubric under which local governments might seek to raise taxes, and under which they should expect resources from central government. The current system is implicitly criticised as overcentralised in terms of tax-raising powers, meaning that local governments are frequently financially disempowered, and lack resources, and thus put under pressure to use unorthodox means to seek funds.

STRENGTHENING CONSULTATIVE BODIES

Hu Jintao has asked for more 'public participation' in decision-making. People's congresses are seen as able to help deliver this. The CCPPC in 1949 grouped together the eight patriotic parties that were allowed to remain in existence, along with government trade unions, and other public bodies – in essence, the coalition of social forces called the 'United Front'. This is now seen as needing an enhanced role in offering feedback on government policy, and legitimising government decision-making among a wider public. The CCPPCs at local and national level should be 'a means of greater democratisation'. In terms of the division of responsibility between people's congresses and CCPPCs, the latter should deal with specialised issues, because they can 'more adequately represent local specific interests than perhaps the people's congresses can'.[55] The CCPPC cannot allow itself to be overtaken by local interests that go against national interests, and therefore once more needs the guidance of the CCP. But it should be a place where bolder, newer policies are discussed; it should be more representative of the complex constituencies that make up the current PRC; and it should have a clear legal status.

LEGAL REFORM

Storming the Fortress identifies four areas where legal reforms now need to be deepened. There must be: (1) clearer relations between the separate levels of law, from local to national level; (2) better administration of the law; (3) commercialisation of law; and (4) the localisation of law, and education of the public about what it can, and cannot, achieve.

The sheer extent of the legal changes in the last three decades has brought about contradictions and anomalies. While in theory laws can originate from the State Council, over 70 per cent are devised by central government ministries, and by local governments, which have the powers to pass laws and 'regulations' (*fagui*) specific to their area. *Storming the Fortress* argues that this system remains lacking in transparency, and needs greater 'openness', with more systematic consultation with the public. The US system is cited approvingly. After the book was published, the new Chinese Employment Law was brought in nationally in January 2008, after an exhaustive process of public consultation, both in writing and within the 2007 NPC. The sheer number of responses to this request for feedback (with over 300,000 separate submissions) has made the government think more about the best and most efficient way to get feedback on draft legislation.

Judges are a particular problem. They lack specialist training, are poorly paid, and are often from a military, governmental or non-specialist background, but are expected to pass judgment on highly technical areas of law. A national system of judge training akin to that operating in Japan needs to be established. In addition, the funding of courts at local and national levels has to be addressed, with systems of legal aid and access to justice studied and set up. The delivery of social justice, as Hu Jintao himself has stated, is critical, especially in one area where the poor quality of judges creates clear collusion between them and local officials: 'Resolutely punishing and effectively preventing corruption bears on popular support for the Party and its very survival.'

ADMINISTRATIVE REFORM

Expert on Chinese law Randy Peerenboom has stated that 'One of [China's] biggest challenges will be to bring the political system more in line with the economic system... The role of the CCP in daily governance needs to be clarified, *with greater separation between the CCP and the state.*'[56] *Storming the Fortress* outlines some of the expansions of the Chinese administrative machinery over the history of the PRC, with major expansions and then retractions of the number of government ministries centrally, and their personnel, over the 1980s and then into the 1990s. The reduction in the number of ministries during the premiership of Zhu Rongji, which was agreed at the NPC in 2001, continued with a more modest further reduction in 2007 and 2008. The clear policy under Jiang Zemin of separating out business and government functions, both in the military and in the government, in 1998–99, was also a significant milestone. Philosophically, limits need to be accepted for the role of government. 'We have', the book's authors explain, 'to change the idea from the past that government has limitless power, and limitless responsibility.'[57] Echoing one of Hu's key slogans, they insist that 'government must put people at its centre'. It needs to be more technical in its mode of management, and avoid the historical perils of overmanagement and bureaucratisation (one of Mao Zedong's great bugbears), and exercise budgetary accountability.

FABRIC OF SOCIETY

According to its constitution, China is a multi-religious society. Attempts to carry out the prescription in Marx to bring about the disappearance of the practice of religion were largely abandoned in the 1980s. The freedom of religious belief is guaranteed by Article 36 of the 1982 Constitution. The authors of *Storming the Fortress* defend this principle, but state that 'religion cannot interfere with national sovereignty and must contribute to social harmony',[58] an oblique reference to the fear of separatism posed by, in particular, religious-nationalist separatist groups in the border areas. The explosion in the number of civil society groups, across the whole range of social activity from trade unions to trade associations, to environmental protection groups, is recognised, along with 'the high concept of service and help to the self-discipline of society' these provide. Civil society groups are able to help improve the quality of government policy, but their relationship with the state must be regulated more closely. The strengthening of the market economy, and of legal foundations for property rights, is seen as a factor which will increase the importance and confidence of civil society. Perhaps somewhat negatively, however, the book's authors state their belief that 'contemporary society has still not developed to the level when religion no longer exists'.[59] In the short to medium term, therefore, the policy should be that religion is tolerated.

General issues

As the authors of *Storming the Fortress* openly state, 'reform carries risks, but so does not reforming'. The crucial issue is to have a plan, a 'step-by-step' vision. They differ from the discourse of political change found in statements by elite political leaders by presenting a specific timeline for when change will need to be introduced, and when completed. Inevitably this is closely tied to economic conditions. From 1978 to 2000, therefore, China saw the creation of 'the primary stage of socialism', creating an economic base. The creation of a middle-income country with 'a moderate level of prosperity' will take until 2020. For the crucial third stage, China will see 'the perfection of its market economy, the appearance of a strong nation, and the increasingly improved quality of Chinese people's lives'. At this point, from 2020 to 2040, China will see the appearance of a 'middle-level democratic and legally modernised country'. This whole process will therefore have taken sixty years in all. China will need to devise its own form of governance, and its own specific form of 'Party-led' democracy, throughout this period, simply because 'representative (Western liberal) democracy is inadequate to deal with the balance of interests in such a complex society [as China].'[60]

This form of Chinese democracy can adopt and adapt certain aspects of models of representative democracy in places like the USA, Europe, Japan and elsewhere: transparency, accountability, public participation in decision-making, and more efficient administration. At the heart of this – and this is a theme that *Storming the Fortress* returns to in almost all its treatments of the separate areas of reform, from the legal to social to administrative – is financial regulation, and the control, scrutiny and approval of budgets. The 'most basic issue in democracy is the financial and tax systems'. If there is to be public trust in government, it must come through the handling of resources and money. A just and equitable division of payments in tax to local and central government, and of receipts and benefits from natural resources, is a critical part of the book's vision; the practical means to deal with this lie at the heart of many of its proposals. This is part of what makes the book, despite the very clear limits (of which more later) of its political blueprint, refreshing – its willingness to offer up practical solutions to some of China's seemingly intractable administrative and institutional challenges.

The authors of *Storming the Fortress* admit, like Hu Jintao, that the Party has problems, but its place in the structure of government in China, and in legitimate political life, remains unchallenged. For this reason, throughout the discussions the book presents, there is a clear line beyond which its proposal does not stray. A full and independent judiciary, for instance, and the opening up of the whole decision-making process to 'the people' through open elections are two clear 'forbiddens'. 'People's choice', the authors state, 'is no guarantee that they will make the right choice'. The limits of representative democracy's ability to satisfy many demands for just and fair treatment of social issues, and the many cases of failure, are matters that have been discussed exhaustively in Western studies. For *Storming the Fortress*, as Liu Xiaobo said in his criticisms of the White Paper on Democracy quoted in Chapter 1, sees the CCP as having a role, and a wisdom, that is almost above society, and offering a guarantee against Chinese society being wrecked on its own internal contradictions and complexities. In the specific areas of information management, for instance, the role of the Party in supplying parameters is clear.

Can it be done?

Storming the Fortress supplies two essential things that have so far been lacking in the elite discourse of political change and reform in the PRC: a narrative and a practical blueprint. For the first, its projection of a sixty-year process towards a kind of democracy, with 2040 set as the end point, at least gives us some sense of the sort of time frame within which change is expected to occur, and the ambitions that are being talked of. Setting this against what appears to be the inherent pessimism of Chinese leaders regarding future options (continuing as we are, muddling through or seeing radical breakdown and change, with the regime, like many of its predecessors in Chinese history, simply blown away), there is at least a deeper sense of what a genuine transition might be like. This narrative is important, as it gives contemporary experiences some meaning and context, showing that they are at least on the way somewhere, and that somewhere is based on a set of defined experiences in the recent past and present. One of the striking features of Hu Jintao's speech at the Seventeenth Party Congress, which supplies the political cover and ideological framework for *Storming the Fortress*, is its lack of specific targets and commitments. In a more politically relaxed atmosphere, many of Hu's grander, more general statements would be held up to practical scrutiny, and to the question of how they were going to be achieved and what they mean. *Storming the Fortress* at least begins this process by looking at very specific changes, like the reduction in the size of people's congresses, the training of judges, the proportion of taxes that can be allocated between central and local government, the layers of administrative government in China and the need for their reduction.

The authors of *Storming the Fortress* stress the need for administrative change above all else. The fundamental system, therefore, remains unchanged, particularly the role of the Party and of the government. This of course lays them open to the simple, but perhaps devastating, criticism that they are merely tinkering around with details of the system, whereas, as Nobel laureate Liu Xiaobo has written, the problem is the system itself. One very specific question concerns accountability, and how the CPC can be, in the end, accountable for both the performance of government and its own internal workings, when there is a clear lack of transparency regarding how it regulates itself, makes personnel decisions, deals with its own finances and disciplines its members. *Storming the Fortress* keeps well clear of this issue, and in that sense sets it up like a worrying black box at the heart of much else that it discusses. Can a non-accountable, self-regulating body like the Party really maintain this system and deal credibly with the other administrative bodies outside of it? Experience elsewhere suggests that this is not possible, and that 'pick and mix' or selective accountability is a chimera.

What the Party does supply, however, is social cohesiveness, and a unifying ideology, where otherwise only disunity might reign. The Party's ability to talk of the pain that disunity brought in recent Chinese history, particularly at the end of the Qing Dynasty up to 1911, and then during the Republican Period until 1949, still have great traction in China. This means that the Party is accorded a highly privileged place, and its role is not questioned. Only the most courageous dissident voices, like Liu Xiaobo's, dare to do this, and they do so, as he was tragically to discover, at their peril.

Finally, *Storming the Fortress* offers only highly benign scenarios for China's short- to mid-term future. Under these circumstances, there will be time and opportunity to deliver the sort of practical changes that the book's authors believe will make life better for Chinese citizens, deal with the ongoing problems of inequality and social injustice, and avoid the historical problems of social instability. For their scenarios, the authors do not look in any detail at internal or external sources of disruption, from a severe economic downturn in China, to a pandemic, to escalating environmental problems that place increasing pressures on society and start to tear away some of its hard-earned current cohesion. Nor is the international context discussed, where tensions or even conflict with outside actors might also blow China's smooth trajectory off course.

In these cases, all bets are off. As a representation of elite thinking on China's future steps towards a reformed political system, *Storming the Fortress* offers much food for thought. But it takes us, in some senses, only to the threshold of a new portal, to a new set of possibilities. It does not take us through, to see what might lie on the other side.

Last words

Even the fiercest opponents of the CCP admit that its rule over the PRC in the last three decades has been ruthlessly pragmatic. The Party's pragmatism and realism have ensured that it was able to combine one-party rule with one of the most dynamic economic explosions the world has seen. Even in the wake of one of the worst economic crises in modern times, China was able to produce 11.5 per cent GDP growth for the first quarter of 2010. This was a time when the rest of the world was crawling back into positive figures after months of negative indices.

This is not the whole story, however. 'GDP rates are simply a measure of productivity', as one financial expert told me in Beijing in May 2010. 'You can simply have the state going around telling people to dig holes in the ground, and say that that is productivity. It is the quality of growth that matters.' The quality of growth is becoming a key issue in China as it gets closer to its aim of being a middle-income society by 2020, with a per capita GDP of US$3,000. In order to do that, a shift needs to be made between simply talking grandly of creating a 'harmonious society', where there is greater social concord, stability and unity, and actually doing things that will bring this about.

Village elections, and the process of rural democracy, matter for many reasons. But the main one is that they occur in a part of the country and in a sector of society which history tells us matter hugely. For most of the past three thousand years China has been an agrarian society. The vast majority of its people have been farmers or worked on the land. Rural China was home to the great rebellions that upset dynasties through the centuries, bringing about change. Mao Zedong's communist revolution in the end sought its support in the countryside, among some of the poorest farmers in the land. They fought in his armies, and in the end they won the wars that brought him to power in 1949. The countryside was the key source of his support, so much so that when confronted in the Great Leap Forward by a backlash within the Party elite, he simply threatened to retreat back to the countryside, establish another arm, and fight a new war for legitimacy.

The Reform and Opening Up era began in the countryside, even though its results were to have huge impact on the urbanisation of China and the shift in population from countryside to city. The reforms in the agricultural sector in the early 1980s meant that millions were freed up for enterprises. China was finally able to feed itself, and to do business. The most isolated parts of the countryside were often the most entrepreneurial. Wenzhou, in coastal Zhejiang province, the capital city of modern-day non-state business people, was without a rail link to the rest of China and had a very poor electricity supply, even into the late 1980s. And yet it now stands as a place with over 100,000 enterprises. The Wenzhou phenomenon has been nationally and internationally studied to understand its mysteries.

Village elections were to accompany the economic reforms in the 1980s. Paradoxically, they were supported in their early years by leaders who were, on most other issues, hardliners. Peng Zhen was the founding patron. He was no liberal, and took a tough stance on most other areas of political reform. But, in this, he believed that the Party had to compromise. Experiments in the early years were rolled out across the country in the 1990s, and an improved legal infrastructure was put in place in 1998. Tentative attempts were made to expand these elections to other areas, within the Party, in townships, even in prefectures. They introduced key concepts into China, like one person, one vote ballots, secret voting and multi-party elections. But in the last ten years, the initial excitement that greeted them, both within and outside China, has been dampened somewhat. No significant moves have been made to expand the principles underlying these elections elsewhere. They remain a largely isolated island in a landscape dominated by CCP centralism and control. And there are plenty of ways in which the CCP has exercised control over even these small enclaves. Many examples have been given in this book, but they are only a small sample.

In fact, rural democracy in China now best makes sense if taken as part of huge social transformation that has created non-governmental groups, a legal sector, and a host of other social forces which are now shaping Chinese society. Economic reforms have unleashed all sorts of other forces, re-creating the contract between the Party and society in ways which, even a decade ago, would have been unimaginable. The Internet now has half a billion users in the country, creating links between different groups, allowing people to express themselves in ways which were once not possible, holding corrupt local and national officials to account through 'lynching' and 'flesh searches', where claims are made, evidence produced and figures pursued. Society is developing at such a rate that tragic and deeply disturbing manifestations of unease, like the series of school stabbings that occurred in early 2010, are only the grimmest manifestation of other deep-seated social and spiritual problems. As a scholar said to me in late 2009, 'Chinese society is in ferment. Things change by the day, by the hour. We can barely keep up.' Another Chinese friend was more prosaic: 'This place is like fairy-land', she said, a little wearily, 'anything can happen here'.

The CCP is the one still point in this moving world, its structures largely unchanged from half a century ago. It supplies unity and some semblance of stability in a world which, for much of the time, appears like a riot. In its calm central halls and power forums the Party asserts a form of control, even if it often looks like firefighting. As this book has tried to show, village elections are connected to the larger debate about democracy in China, and that is connected to a whole constellation of issues, from building the rule of law, to creating civil society, to the very issue of legitimacy of the CCP itself. As novelist E.M. Forster famously commented, 'Only connect.' It is a relatively short mental journey from the ballot boxes used in some of the most isolated parts of the PRC to the halls of power in Beijing. There is a link between how governance is delivered in the countryside and how secure the CCP is in Beijing.

And there is finally the question of good faith. Have elections at the village level been a huge sop for people, giving them a sense of power when, in fact, things remain just as they were, with the elite in Beijing thoroughly in control? Are they in fact real, important social experiments, with perhaps – one day – massive relevance to the development of Chinese society? Are they a genuine space in which some of the great conflicts and contradictions of contemporary Chinese society are able to play out against each other? Do they contain the potential seeds of a huge revolutionary change?

Elections are probably part of all of these. I have tried to show in this book some of the rich discussion, debate and argument that are taking place about where China should be going, as it stands on the verge of a major elite leadership change in 2012, and enters the second decade of the twenty-first century – a century that many have claimed will uniquely be shaped by, and belong to, China. The beauty of village elections is that they capture many of these huge issues manageably, and in a very local context and area. They reveal much of what is good and bad about the PRC, and convey much of the excitement as it remakes itself; and they give us an insight into the Party that is in charge of the country, including its own crucial mission to stay in power. Village elections might well be a gift from the past, but they might just yet offer a small peek into the future. And for that, they deserve to be studied.

Notes

INTRODUCTION

1. Constitution of the PRC 1982, at http://english.peopledaily.com.cn/constitution/constitution.html; accessed 9 August 2010.

CHAPTER 1

1. See William T. Rowe, *The Great Qing*, Belknap Press, Cambridge MA, 2009, p. 127.
2. Kang Youwei and Liang Qichao were both key liberal reformers who were active in the final years of the Qing Dynasty from 1880 to 1911. Kang was a prolific author, on matters from social reform to political issues. Liang wrote widely on China's engagement with the outside world. Both were intimately associated with the doomed Hundred Days Reform Movement in the late 1890s, where proposals for fundamental changes to the imperial system that ruled China for centuries were set out, only to be summarily dismissed by the reigning powers in Beijing.
3. Immanuel C.Y. Hsu, *The Rise of Modern China*, 6th edn, Oxford University Press, Oxford, 2000, pp. 477–8.
4. Frank Dikötter, *The Age of Openness: China Before Mao*, Hong Kong University Press, Hong Kong, 2008, p. 7.
5. Ibid., pp. 18–19.
6. Ibid., pp. 20–23.
7. Qiusha Ma, *Non-Governmental Organizations in Contemporary China: Paving the Way to Civil Society*, Routledge, London, 2006, p. 33.
8. Ibid., p. 37.
9. Ibid., p. 45.

10. Ibid., p. 38.

11. Rana Mitter, *A Bitter Revolution: China's Struggle with the Modern World*, Oxford University Press, Oxford, 2004, p. 3.

12. Ibid., pp. 14–15.

13. W.H. Auden and Christopher Isherwood, *Journey to a War*, Faber & Faber, London, 1939, p. 242.

14. Cited in Paul French, *Through the Looking Glass: China's Foreign Journalists from Opium War to Mao*, Hong Kong University Press, Hong Kong, 2009, p. 202.

15. See ibid., pp. 203–4.

16. Chen Jian, 'The Chinese Liberation of Tibet 1949–51' in Jeremy Brown and Paul Pickowicz, eds, *Dilemmas of Victory: The Early Years of the People's Republic of China*, Harvard University Press, Cambridge MA, 2007, p. 131.

17. Mao Zedong, 'On New Democracy', at www.marxists.org/reference/archive/mao/selected-works/volume-2/mswv2_26.htm; accessed 29 March 2010.

18. Ibid.

19. This era in the recent history of the CCP is covered in Kerry Brown, *Friends and Enemies: The Past, Present and Future of the Communist Party of China*, Anthem Press, London, 2009.

20. Roderick Macfarquhar and Michael Schoenhals, *Mao's Last Revolution*, Belknap Press, Cambridge MA, 2006, p. 458.

21. Ibid., p. 460.

22. Zheng Yi, *Scarlet Memorial: Tales of Cannibalism in Modern China*, Harper-Collins, London and New York, 1997.

23. Ralph A. Thaxton, *Catastrophe and Contention in Rural China: Mao's Great Leap Forward Famine and the Origins of Righteous Resistance in Da Fo Village*, Cambridge University Press, Cambridge, 2008, p. 24.

24. Ibid., p. 90.

25. Ibid., p. 216.

26. Ibid., p. 301.

27. Yang Jisheng's *Mubei* (Tombstone), a monumental two-volume Chinese-language account of the Great Leap Forward and the famines, which appeared in 2008, is only available in Hong Kong and Taiwan at present.

28. Thaxton, *Catastrophe and Contention in Rural China*, p. 301.

29. Song Yongyi, 'The End of Innocence: Heterodox Thought on Human Rights and Political Reform during the Cultural Revolution', at Human Rights in China, www.hrichina.org/public/contents/article?revision_id=3148&item_id=3147; accessed 29 March 2010.

30. The full text of this anti-revisionist masterpiece can be found at www.wenge-wang.org/read.php?tid=4985&keyword=zhang; accessed 29 March 2010.

31. Gao Wenqian, *Zhou Enlai: The Last Perfect Revolutionary*, Public Affairs, New York, 2007, p. 275.

32. Cited in 'Wei Jingsheng: My Life for Democracy', *Share Magazine*, June 1998, at www.share-international.org/ARCHIVES/political/po_Wei_Jingsheng.htm.

33. Li Lanqing, *Breaking Through: The Birth of China's Opening-up Policy*, Oxford University Press, Oxford, 2009, p. 70.
34. Zhao Ziyang, *Prisoner of State: The Secret Journal of Premier Zhao Ziyang*, Simon & Schuster, New York, 2009.
35. Li Lanqing, *Breaking Through*, pp. 14–15.
36. Cited in Yasheng Huang, *Selling China*, Cambridge University Press, Cambridge, 2003, p. 308.

CHAPTER 2

1. Hu Jintao: 'Hold High the Great Banner of Socialism with Chinese Characteristics and Strive for New Victories in Building a Moderately Prosperous Society in All Respects', Report to the 17th National Congress, 15 October 2007, issued in English translation by Xinhua News Agency.
2. Liu Xiaobo and others, 'China's Charter 08', trans. Perry Link, *New York Review of Books*, 15 January 2009, at www.nybooks.com/articles/22210; accessed 1 April 2010.
3. Cited in John Thornton, 'Long Time Coming: The Prospects for Democracy in China', *Foreign Affairs*, January/February 2008, p. 3.
4. Ibid., p. 3.
5. John Keane, *The Life and Death of Democracy*, Simon & Schuster, London, 2009, p. xv.
6. Yu Keping, *Democracy is a Good Thing: Essays on Politics, Society and Culture in Contemporary China*, Brookings Institute, Washington DC, 2009, p. 3.
7. Yu Jianrong, speech at the Chinese Council of Lawyers, 26 December 2009, at www.chinaelections.org/Newsinfo.asp?NewsID=169507; accessed 20 March 2010.
8. In 2007, the central government stopped collecting data on mass incidents, which is why the later figures Yu Jianrong used, referred to above, are merely estimates.
9. Guobin Yang, *The Power of the Internet in China: Citizen Activism Online*, Columbia University Press, New York, 2009, p. 25.
10. *Liu ge Weishenme* [The Six Whys], People's Daily Publishing House, Beijing, 2009, p. 7.
11. Ibid., p. 10.
12. Ibid., p. 19.
13. Ibid., p. 20.
14. Ibid., p. 34.
15. Ibid., p. 37.
16. Constitution of the PRC 1982, from http://english.peopledaily.com.cn/constitution/constitution.html; accessed 9 August 2009.
17. Ibid., p. 49.
18. Ibid., p. 56.
19. Ibid., p. 65.
20. Ibid., p. 72.

21. Ibid., p. 75.
22. Frank N. Pieke, *The Good Communist: Elite Training and State Building in Today's China*, Cambridge University Press, Cambridge, 2009, p. 121.
23. Zhou Tianyong, Wang Changjiang and Wang Anling, eds, *Gong Jian, Zhong-guo Zhengzhi Tizhi Gaige Yanjiu Bao Gao, Shi Qi Da Hou* [*Storming the Fortress: A Report on the Reform of China's Political System after the 17th Party Congress*], Xinjiang Production Corps Publication House, Xinjiang, 2007.
24. Ibid., p. 4.
25. Ibid., p. 7.
26. Ibid.
27. Ibid., p. 19.
28. State Council Information Office, *Building of Political Democracy in China*, issued 2007, Preface, at www.china.org.cn/english/features/book/145941.htm; accessed 8 April 2010.
29. John Wilson Lewis, *Leadership in Communist China*, Cornell University Press, New York, 1963, p. 74.
30. Ibid., p. 75.
31. Ibid., p. 76.
32. Ibid., p. 79.
33. Ibid., p. 266.
34. Pan Wei, 'Towards a Consultative Rule of Law Regime in China', in Suisheng Zhao, ed., *Debating Political Reform in China: Rule of Law vs. Democratization*, M.E. Sharpe, Armonk NY, 2006, p. 5.
35. Ibid., p. 7.
36. Ibid., p. 8.
37. Ibid., p. 10.
38. Ibid., p. 12.
39. Ibid., p. 17.
40. Ibid., p. 20.
41. Ibid., p. 29.
42. Ibid., p. 34.
43. Ibid., p. 40.
44. Ibid., p. 3.
45. For an early assessment of this in the Hu-Wen administration, see Willy Lam, 'Chinese Corruption Crusade Causes New Factional Infighting', *China Brief*, vol. 4, no. 2, March 2004, at www.jamestown.org/single/?no_cache=1&tx_ttnews[tt_news]=26230; accessed 21 March 2010.
46. There are good arguments to say that Chen was felled more for political reasons (he opposed Premier Wen Jiabao on a couple of key economic policies in the months before his downfall) than for any real issue of corruption.
47. Provinces include Taiwan. Lai Hairong, 'Semi Competitive Elections at Township Level in Sichuan Province', *China Perspectives*, January–February 2004, http://chinaperspectives.revues.org/document 787.html.
48. This section is based on papers obtained in Beijing in August 2009.
49. Xinhua report, 17 July 2009, personal archive of author.

CHAPTER 3

1. Zhang Chunqiao, 'On Exercising All Round Dictatorship of the Bourgeoisie', at www.marxists.org/reference/archive/zhang/1975/x01/x01.htm; accessed 22 April 2010.
2. Liu Heung Shing, ed., *China: Portrait of a Country*, Taschen, Hong Kong and New York, 2008, pp. 264–5.
3. Deng Xiaoping, 'Emancipate the Mind, Seek Truth From Facts, Unite as One in Looking to the Future', speech on 13 December 1978, at http://web.peopledaily.com.cn/english/dengxp/vol2/text/b1260.html.
4. Barry Naughton, *The Chinese Economy: Transition and Growth*, MIT Press, Cambridge MA, 2007, p. 115.
5. Shi Tianjian, *Rural Democracy in China*, World Scientific Publishing, Singapore, 2000, p. 10.
6. 'Constitution of the People's Republic of China', adopted on 4 December 1982, at http://english.peopledaily.com.cn/constitution/constitution.html.
7. See Amy B. Epstein, 'Village Elections in China: Experimentation with Democracy', in E. Bliney, *Crisis and Reform in China*, Nova Science Publishers, Hauppauge NY, 1997, p. 138.
8. Interview, Beijing, August 2009 and July 2009.
9. Interview, Beijing, 4 August 2009.
10. Interview, Beijing, 4 August 2009.
11. Text of first law available at www.86148.com/englishlaw/shownews.asp?id=129.
12. Yasheng Huang, *Capitalism with Chinese Characteristics: Entrepreneurship and the State*, Cambridge University Press, Cambridge, 2008, p. 51.
13. Chen Guidi and Wu Chuntao, *Will the Boat Sink the River: The Life of China's Peasant*, Public Affairs, London and New York, 2006, p. 151.
14. See Sherlyn WuDunn, 'China's Growing Discontent with Taxes on the Peasants', *New York Times*, 19 May 1993.
15. Chen and Wu, *Will the Boat Sink the River*, p. 89. Many more cases of unrest in the 1990s are dealt with in Thomas P. Bernstein, 'Unrest in Rural China: A 2003 Assessment', Center for Study of Democracy, University of California, Irvine, 2004.
16. The full law is available in translation at www.china.org.cn/english/government/207279.htm; accessed 10 April 2010.
17. Interview, Beijing, August 2009.
18. Based on interviews (names and locations changed) in China in summer 2009.
19. Goran Leijonhufvud, 'Village Elections in Minority Nationalities Areas', paper prepared for the Norwegian Centre for Human Rights, Oslo, 2006. I am grateful to the author for supplying me with this and another paper relating to village elections.
20. Linda Jakobson, 'Local Governance: Village and Township Direct Elections', in Jude Howell, ed., *Governance in China*, Rowan & Littlefield, Oxford, 2004, p. 104.

21. Joseph Fewsmith, *The Political Economy of China's Transition*, Foundation for Law Justice and Society, and the Centre for Socio-Legal Studies, University of Oxford, 2008, p. 6. I am also grateful for information in Jacques De Lisle, 'What's Happened to Democracy in China?', at www.fpri.org.

22. Simon Shen, 'Disharmony at the Grassroots Level: Possible Alienation Caused by Town-Level Direct Elections in China', *Journal of Chinese Political Science* 15, 2010, p. 192.

23. 'Direct Elections Move to Township Level', *China Daily*, 18 May 2004, at www. chinadaily.com.cn/english/doc/2004-05/18/content_331594.htm.

24. Lai Hairong, 'Semi-Competitive Elections at Township Level in Sichuan Province', *China Perspectives*, January–February 2004, at http://chinaperspectives. revues.org/document787.html.

25. Shen, 'Disharmony at the Grassroots Level', p. 194.

26. 'Shenzhen: Competitive Election of Party, Government Chiefs to be Introduced in Bold Political Reform', 26 May 2010, at http://english.peopledaily. com.cn/90001/90776/90785/6999424.html.

27. Carter Center Delegation Report, 'Village Elections In China', 5 March 1997, at www.cartercenter.org/documents/1155.pdf.

28. Mao Zedong, 'On Contradiction', in *Selected Works*, Foreign Languages Press, Beijing.

29. Fubing Su and Dali Yang, 'Elections, Governance and Accountability in Rural China', *Asian Perspectives*, vol. 29, no. 4, 2005, p. 153.

30. Li Fan, *Zhongguo Jiceng Minzhu Fazhan Bao Gao 2009* [Report on the Development of Primary Level Democracy in China, 2009], Huawen Publishers, Beijing, 2009, pp. 3–6.

31. Jonathan Watts, *When A Billion Chinese Jump*, Faber & Faber, London, 2010.

32. A tragically typical example, from a letter by a female prison inmate to Beria, the head of the security apparatus under Stalin in the late 1930s, is cited in Dmitri Volkogonov, *Stalin: Triumph and Tragedy*, Grove Weidenfeld, New York, 1988: 'I have been living all these years in the camps and have kept the belief that truth and justice would conquer lies and injustice in our country.' As Volkogonov curtly states, 'Beria simply confirmed the sentence without taking further action' (p. 335).

33. Profile and interview, *Time* magazine, 8 March 2004, pp. 30ff.; and Li Fan, 'China's Unquiet Countryside', *Time* magazine, 24 October 2005, p. 56.

CHAPTER 4

1. Steven Mosher, 'Are the Chinese Ready for Liberty and Self-Government', *The American Enterprise*, vol. 9, no. 4, July–August 1998, pp. 50–53.

2. Baogong He, *Rural Democracy in China: The Role of Village Elections*, Palgrave Macmillan, Basingstoke, 2007, pp. 53–4.

3. He, p. 56.

4. He, p. 59.

5. He, p. 62.
6. Ray Huang, *1587: A Year of No Significance*, Yale University Press, New Haven CT, 1981, p. 1.
7. Yan'an, in central China, was the final destination for the Communists' long march in 1935–36, and served as their base during the war against the Japanese, and the Civil War from 1946 to 1949.

CHAPTER 5

1. Hu Chuanqi, 'China Modernisation Report 2009', at www.modernization.com.cn/cmr2009%20overview.htm.
2. Wang Xiaodong, Song Shaojun, Huang Jilao and Song Qiang, eds, *Zhongguo Bu Gaoxing* [China is Not Happy], Phoenix Publishing, Jiangsu People's Publishing Company, Nanjing, 2009.
3. Ibid., p. 13.
4. Ibid., p. 31.
5. Ibid., p. 33.
6. Ibid., p. 34.
7. Ibid., p. 77.
8. Ibid., p. 81.
9. Ibid., p. 87.
10. Ibid., p. 92.
11. Ibid., p. 96.
12. Ibid., p. 99.
13. Ibid., p. 101.
14. Ibid., p. 103.
15. Ibid., p. 146.
16. Steve Tsang, 'Consultative Leninism: China's New Political Framework', *Journal of Contemporary China* 18, November 2009, p. 866.
17. Ibid.
18. See 'Eight Pupils Stabbed to Death in Chinese School', BBC News online, 24 March 2010, at http://news.bbc.co.uk/1/hi/world/asia-pacific/8582203.stm; accessed 12 July 2010.
19. Xiaoyang Wang, 'The Post Communist Type Man', *China Journal*, January 2002.
20. Kenneth Lieberthal and David M. Lampton, eds, *Bureaucracy, Politics and Decision-Making in Post-Mao China*, University of California Press, Berkeley, 1992.
21. Vivienne Shue, *The Reach of the State*, Stanford University Press, Stanford CA, 1988, p. 79.
22. *Cambridge History of China*, Volume 12, Cambridge University Press, Cambridge, 1983, p. 526.
23. Liang Jing, 'Yichang weihu rende liangzhi yu zunyan de baowei zhan' ['A Battle to Preserve Human Conscience and Dignity'], *Xin shiji* [New Age Magazine] 12 January 2010. Translation by David Kelly.

24. Paper on Criminal Law Developments on China, passed to Kerry Brown on 10 May 2010.
25. Joseph Kahn, 'Chinese Official Warns against Independence of Courts', *New York Times*, 3 February 2007, at www.nytimes.com/2007/02/03/world/asia/03china.html?_r=1&ex=157680000&en=0d4e8750660343a2&ei=5124&partner=permalink&exprod=permalink.
26. Pan Wei, 'Towards a Consultative Rule of Law Regime in China', in Suisheng Zhao, ed., *Debating Political Reform in China: Rule of Law versus Democratization*, M.E. Sharpe, New York, 2006. pp. 3–40
27. Part of this has been taken from Kerry Brown, 'Gao Zhisheng and China's Question', *Open Democracy*, 3 February 2010, at www.opendemocracy.net/kerry-brown/gao-zhisheng-and-chinas-question.
28. Gao Zhisheng, *A China More Just*, Broad Press, New York, 2007.
29. Gao Zhisheng, 'Dark Night, Dark Hood, and Kidnapping by Dark Mafia: My Account of More Than 50 Days Torture in 2007', Human Rights Watch, at http://hrichina.org/public/PDFs/PressReleases/2009.02.08_Gao_Zhisheng_account_ENG.pdf.
30. Interview, Beijing, May 2010.
31. Interview, *International Institutional Investor*, April 2010, pp. 34–5.
32. Yasheng Huang's book, *Capitalism with Chinese Characteristics* (Cambridge University Press, Cambridge, 2008) deals at length with the highly state-orientated nature of Shanghai's economy.
33. *China Statistical Yearbook, 2008*, China Statistics Press, Beijing, 2009, p. 932.
34. www.gjxfj.gov.cn/.
35. Cited in *China: An Alleyway in Hell: China's Abusive Black Jails*, Human Rights Watch Report, New York, 2009.
36. Cara Anna, 'American Woman Becomes Petitioner in China', Associated Press, 1 December 2009, at www.signonsandiego.com/news/2009/dec/01/american-woman-becomes-petitioner-in-china/.
37. See Zhang Ye, 'China's Emerging Civil Society', Brookings Institution, Washington DC, 2003, at www.brookings.edu/~/media/Files/rc/papers/2003/08china_ye/ye2003.pdf.
38. Elizabeth Economy, *The River Runs Black*, Council on Foreign Relations, Cornell University, Ithaca NY, 2005, ch. 5.
39. Robert Saiget, 'China Environmentalist Alleges Brutal Jail Treatment', AFP, 11 May, at http://news.yahoo.com/s/afp/20100511/wl_asia_afp/chinaenvironmentpollutionrights.
40. 'Women's Rights NGO Responds to Cancellation by Peking University', at www.hrichina.org/public/contents/press?revision_id=173547& item_id=173519.
41. Peter Ford, 'Another Aids Activist Wan Yanhai, Flees China', *Christian Science Monitor*, 10 May 2010, at www.csmonitor.com/World/Asia-Pacific/2010/0510/Another-AIDS-activist-Wan-Yanhai-flees-China.
42. Neil Munro, 'Democracy Postponed: Chinese Learning from the Soviet Collapse', *China Aktuell* 4, 2008, p. 42.

43. Ibid., p. 44.
44. Details from 'Human Rights Chronology: China, Hong Kong, Tibet', November to December 1998, at www.hrw.org/campaigns/china-98/chron398.htm.
45. BBC Monitoring, April 2010.
46. Richard McGregor, *The Party: The Secret World of China's Communist Rulers*, Allen Lane, London, 2010, pp. 139–40.
47. Cheng Li, 'Intra Party Democracy in China: Should we Take it Seriously', *China Leadership Monitor* 30, Brookings Institute, Washington DC, October 2009, at www.brookings.edu/~/media/Files/rc/papers/2009/fall_china_democracy_li/fall_china_democracy_li.pdf, pp. 1–2.
48. Zhou Tianyong, Wang Changjiang and Wang Anling, eds, *Gong Jian, Zhongguo Zhengzhi Tizhi Gaige Yanjiu Bao Gao, Shi Qi Da Hou* [*Storming the Fortress: A Report on the Reform of China's Political System after the 17th Party Congress*], Xinjiang Production Corps Publication House, Xinjiang, 2007, p. 1.
49. Ibid., p. 4.
50. Ibid., p. 7.
51. Ibid., p. 19.
52. Ibid., p. 47.
53. Lynn T. White, *Political Booms: Local Money and Power in Taiwan, East China, Thailand, and the Philippines*, World Scientific Publishing, Singapore, 2009, p. 51.
54. Archie Brown, *The Rise and Fall of Communism*, Bodley Head, London, 2009, p. 449.
55. Zhou, Wang and Wang, eds, *Gong Jian* [*Storming the Fortress*], p. 115.
56. Randall Peerenboom, *China Modernizes: Threat to the West or Model for the Rest?*, Oxford University Press, Oxford, 2007, p. 284; stress added.
57. Zhou, Wang and Wang, eds, *Gong Jian* [*Storming the Fortress*], p. 162.
58. Ibid., p. 305.
59. Ibid., p. 319.
60. Ibid., p. 122.

Bibliography

One of the earliest and most complete studies of ideas about democracy in the PRC is contained in American sinologist Andrew Nathan's *Chinese Democracy* (University of California Press, 1986). This covers in particular the big character posters that were put up during the Cultural Revolution, with the rebellious groups (Red Guards) that sponsored them, and the outpouring of anger and feeling in the Democracy Wall Movement in 1978–79. This and Jonathan Spence's *The Gate of Heavenly Peace: The Chinese and Their Revolution* (Penguin, 1982) offer the best overviews of the early democratic and political movements from the fall of the Qing Dynasty in 1911–12 to the 1980s and the clampdown on intellectuals mounted during the latter decade. Ralph A. Thaxton, *Catastrophe and Contention in Rural China: Mao's Great Leap Forward Famine and the Origins of Righteous Resistance in Da Fo Village* (Cambridge University Press, 2008) is essential reading on the true situation in the countryside during the great famines of the 1960s, and answers some of the questions about why, two decades later, the countryside needed to be pacified and villagers enfranchised. On the structures of governance in contemporary China, the most succinct and authoritative overview is contained in Anthony Saich, *Governance and Politics of China* (Palgrave Macmillan, 2nd edn, 2004).

On the history of village elections, and their development, the most complete study so far is Baogang He, *Rural Democracy in China: The Role of Village Elections* (Palgrave Macmillan, 2007). The work of Kevin O'Brien offers much more detailed, specialist analysis – in particular the essay co-authored with Liangjiang Li, 'Accommodating "Democracy" in a One Party State: Introducing Village Elections in China', *China Quarterly* 162, pp. 465–89. *The Journal of Chinese Political Science* 15, 2010, has a series of essays on village elections, township elections and other forms of democratic political experiments in contemporary China. In addition, an early overview of where the experiment began, and where it might be significant, is contained in Linda Jakobson, 'Local Governance: Village and Township Direct Elections', in Jude Howell, ed., *Governance in China*, Rowan & Littlefield, Oxford, 2004, p. 104.

One of the best Internet resources on village elections can be found at the Carter Center-run website, http://en.chinaelections.org/ (there is also a parallel Chinese-language website).

For those who can read Chinese, the most complete set of data so far assembled on the whole process of rural democracy can be found in the *Quanguo Cunmin Weiyuanhui Xuanju Gongzuo Jinzhan Baogao* [Work Progress Report on the Complete Chinese Village Committee Elections], Chinese Social Sciences Press, Beijing, 2008. Li Fan at the World China Institute has produced excellent annual surveys of elections in the past decade. His *Jiedu Zhongguo Minzhu* [Understanding Chinese Democracy], World China Institute, Beijing, 2009, is a summary of his experiences promoting democracy at the grassroots level in China.

Index